THE AVIATION WORKSHOP PUBLICATIONS L...
SPOTLIGHT NO.1
DASSAULT MIRAGE F1

by Mark Attrill and Mark Rolfe

FOREWORD

The Dassault Mirage F1 marked a significant departure in design for Marcel Dassault who had, during the 1950s and 1960s, concentrated on the production of a series of elegant delta-winged fighter aircraft with the Mirage III/IV and 5 series. The Mirage F1, by contrast, sported a more traditional high wing with separate tail surfaces inherited from the moribund Mirage G variable geometry aircraft project that had previously been abandoned.

In spite of several early setbacks, including the failure to secure the highly publicised and controversial 1970s 'Sale of the Century' to European NATO nations, eventually won by the General Dynamics F-16 Fighting Falcon, the Mirage F1 series of aircraft did go on to achieve export success and much more. The aircraft has served in large numbers with the French *Armée de l'Air*, where it has enjoyed a second lease of life as a highly effective strike, attack and tactical reconnaissance aircraft after a distinguished career in the air-defence role. No less than ten other countries, most notably in Europe and the Middle East, have also operated the aircraft.

The Mirage F1 has also enjoyed considerable operational success in a wide range of roles in an equally wide variety of theatres. The South African Air Force was almost certainly the first air arm to use the Mirage F1 in anger during the protracted 'Bush War' with Angola, before Iraq and then Ecuador employed the aircraft in conflicts with their respective neighbours during the early 1980s. During this time, the French *Armée de l'Air* used the aircraft extensively in both Central and in North Africa. Morocco and Libya also joined the list of air forces to experience the utility of this extremely versatile multi-role combat aircraft in an operational environment. Since then the the *Armée de l'Air* has used upgraded variants to great effect during UN air operations over the Balkans and, most recently, on NATO operations over Kosovo during the air campaign of 1999.

As some air arms have retired their aircraft, either voluntarily or through financial necessity, others have embarked on modernisation programmes which will guarantee that this elegant French design will remain in service for some time yet. The Mirage F1C enjoyed thirty years of service with the French *Armée de l'Air* in 2003 and its more modern sub-variants are expected to extend this milestone by at least a decade whilst Ecuador, Morocco and Spain have all continued to invest in the aircraft's future with their respective air arms.

Mark Attrill – November 2006

First published in Great Britain in 2006 by The Aviation Workshop Publications Ltd. and Gary Madgwick
13 Charlton Road, Wantage, Oxon, OX12 8EP, UK
Tel: 01235 769038   Fax: 01235 771432
Email: aviation-workshop@btconnect.com
Website: www.theaviationworkshop.co.uk

Copyright 2006 The Aviation Workshop Publications Ltd

All rights reserved. Apart from any fair dealings for the purpose of research, criticism, private study or review, as permitted under the Copyright, Design & Patents Act 1988, no part of this publication may be reproduced, stored in a retrieval system, or transmitted in any form or by any means, electronical, mechanical, chemical, optical, photo-copying, digital copying or photography, recording or otherwise, without the consent in writing of the publishers, The Aviation Workshop Publications Ltd.

Artwork is copyright Mark Rolfe and The Aviation Workshop Publications Ltd 2006.

Managing Editor Gary Madgwick
Cover Design Artwork Mark Rolfe
Layout and design by AMR Design Ltd.
Kestrel Court, Vyne Road, Sherborne St John, Basingstoke, Hants, RG24 9HJ
Tel: 01256 889455   Fax: 01256 889430
www.amrdesign.com

Printed in England by PHP Litho Printers Ltd.
Hoyle Mill, Barnsley, South Yorkshire, S71 1HN

ISBN 1-904643-10-8

Distribution and marketing in UK by The Aviation Workshop Publications Ltd.
Trade terms available on request.

The Globe is a registered trademark to the Aviation Workshop Publications Ltd.

All enquires regarding this publication, past publications or future projects and publications should be directed to the publishers.

Every effort has been made to trace the copyright holders of all photographic material and we apologise in advance for any unintentional omissions. We would be pleased to insert the appropriate acknowledgement in any subsequent edition of this publication.

(Front cover photo: Courtesy Philippe Conquet/*EC1/12*)

1 Operators
pages 2–32

2 Mirage F1 at War
pages 33–43

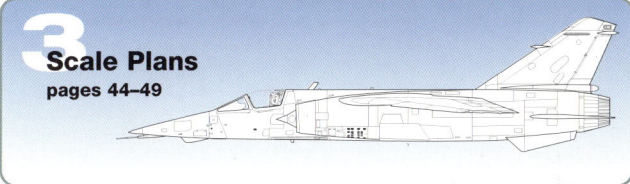

3 Scale Plans
pages 44–49

4 Special Colour Schemes
pages 50–59

5 In Detail
pages 60–79

Publisher's Note

In preparing this book, we have always tried to work from colour photographs and visiting the air bases where possible to confirm markings and serial numbers, etc. In the few instances where this has not been possible and where photographs have not been available, great care has been taken to cross reference all available data and research material.

A very special thanks to the following for their help with this book:

Chris Lofting; Lindsay Peacock; Uli Metternich; Jon Freeman; Paul Dubois (South Africa); Rogier Westerhuis (Aero Images); Seraio Echevria Garcia (Spain); Makis Galiatsatos (Greece); Adrian Balch; Marc Brouyere; Frank C. Duarte; Glenn Sands; Denis J. Calvert; Squadron Leader (now Wing Commander) Dean 'Deano' Andrew MA RAF, *JaBoG 32/1* (1996-98); Wing Commander Andy Kime RAF; Squadron Leader Dave Lord RAF, OC74 (F) Sqn (1994–1995); Capitaine Didier Cohendet, *EC5/330*; Capitaine Theo Fontaine, *EC5/330*: Major General Peter Berger, Director Operations, South African Air Force; Lieutenant Colonel Gerry Wise, South African Air Force; Warrant Officer 2 Alan Taylor, South African Air Force Museum; *Escadron 142, Ala de Caza 14, Ejercito del Air*; Gert Weckx; Sander Smit; Stuart Haigh; Kostas D. Pantios, Jim Smithe/AirPress Photos and Emiel Bonte.

Notes: All photographs by Mark P. Attrill unless otherwise credited.

In addition we would also like to acknowledge the following organisations that have been used as additional reference sources in this publication:

NATO Tiger Meet Associations; www.airliners.net; Scramble on the Web; French Air Force Web Site; South African Air Force Web Site; Martin Baker Ltd, BA Systems Ltd; Zotz Decals, Albatross Decals, Modeldecals (Hannants) and Model Alliance Decals.

In most cases aircraft were finished in Dassault colours as specified by the customer. Those colours quoted in the text therefore relate to the nearest equivalent FS numbers unless otherwise stated. Please check your references for confirmation.

Gary Madgwick – November 2006

Mirage F1 Operators – France

French Air Force (Armée de l'Air)

The origins of the Dassault Mirage F1 family of conventional fighter aircraft can almost certainly be traced back to the development of a combat aircraft known as the Anglo-French Variable Geometry (AFVG), which was sought after the cancellation of the British TSR-2 project in 1965. The British Aircraft Corporation (BAC) and Dassault, working in conjunction with Rolls-Royce and SNECMA, the French engine manufacturer, developed a single-engined variable geometry aircraft known as the Mirage G, which first flew in November 1967, some five months after the French government had unilaterally pulled out of the AFVG programme. In spite of early setbacks, including the loss of the single Mirage G prototype in 1971, Dassault saw the potential for a deep penetration aircraft and developed the twin-engined G8 with a Cyrano IV multi-purpose radar and low-altitude navigation/attack system. For a while, the G8 was touted as a potential competitor to the tri-national MRCA (later Panavia Tornado) being developed by Britain, Germany and Italy. When it became obvious that the MRCA would proceed, France determined that its main requirement was for a fixed-wing design, based on the G8, under the project name ACF (*Avion de Combat Futur*). By 1975, the entire G8/ACF project had been abandoned. Working in parallel with the G8 project, Dassault had fortuitously developed a fixed-geometry Mirage, based on the G8 design and known as the IIIF2, which was an officially sponsored testbed for the new SNECMA TF-306 turbofan. The two-seat IIIF2, which featured a high wing and low tailplane, had first flown in June 1966 and at one time was envisaged to fill the gap between the Mirage IIIs then in service with the *Armée de l'Air* and any new variable-geometry aircraft, before it too was abandoned in the late 1960s.

In the meantime, Dassault had been conducting a private venture to seek a possible replacement for the Mirage III/5 class of fighter with which it had enjoyed considerable domestic and export success. The project effectively scaled down the IIIF2 to roughly the size of its first generation Mirage aircraft using an uprated Atar 9K engine whilst retaining the original aircraft design's full range of high lift devices. The Cyrano IV radar, which provided both air interception and secondary air-to-ground capabilities, was also retained. It soon became clear that

Dassault Mirage F1 prototype (c/n 02) seen at Le Bourget in 1969 in its natural metal finish. Noteworthy are the plain tail surfaces, large roundels and the Mirage F1 motif, in black and yellow on the nose surfaces. (Photo: Lindsay Peacock)

Early production Dassault Mirage F1 photographed at Le Bourget in June 1973. Note the application of the standard *Armée de l'Air* Blue-Grey/Silver camouflage scheme with large national markings, the Le Bourget Show number '1' on the forward fuselage side and the large ejection seat markings applied to the sides of the air intake. (Photo: Lindsay Peacock)

A rather clean looking Mirage F1C 30-MG/38 of *Escadron de Chasse* (EC) 2/3 'Normandie Niemen', which attended the 1987 Open Day at RAF Binbrook. The aircraft wears the original Blue Grey (FS 25189)/Matt aluminium colour scheme that is associated with early service with the *Armée de l'Air* and the fin has yet to be adorned with any of the fairings that were gradually introduced to some aircraft during a number of upgrade programmes.

Dassault Mirage F1C, 330-AC, No.31, operated by *EC5/330* 'Cote d'Argent', based at Mont de Marsan. Aircraft carries an experimental low infra-red reflection scheme.

Reference: *Check List No.1, AMD-BA Mirage F1, DTU:* page 27

Another early *Armée de l'Air* Mirage F1C, this time from *EC1/12* 'Cambresis' at Cambrai/Epinoy, is captured cleaning up its undercarriage on departure from the International Air Tattoo at RAF Fairford in July 1991.

Insignia of *EC5/330* 'Cote d'Argent'

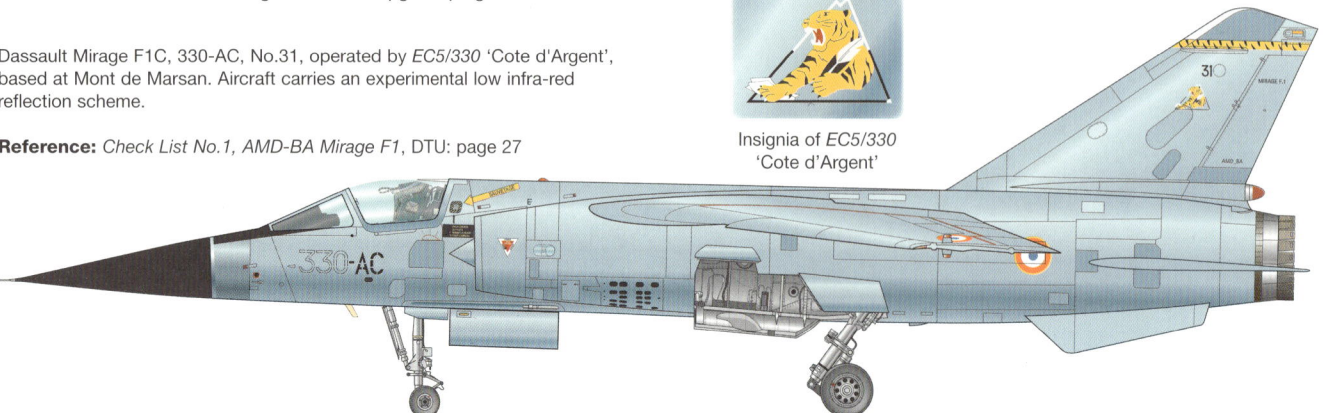

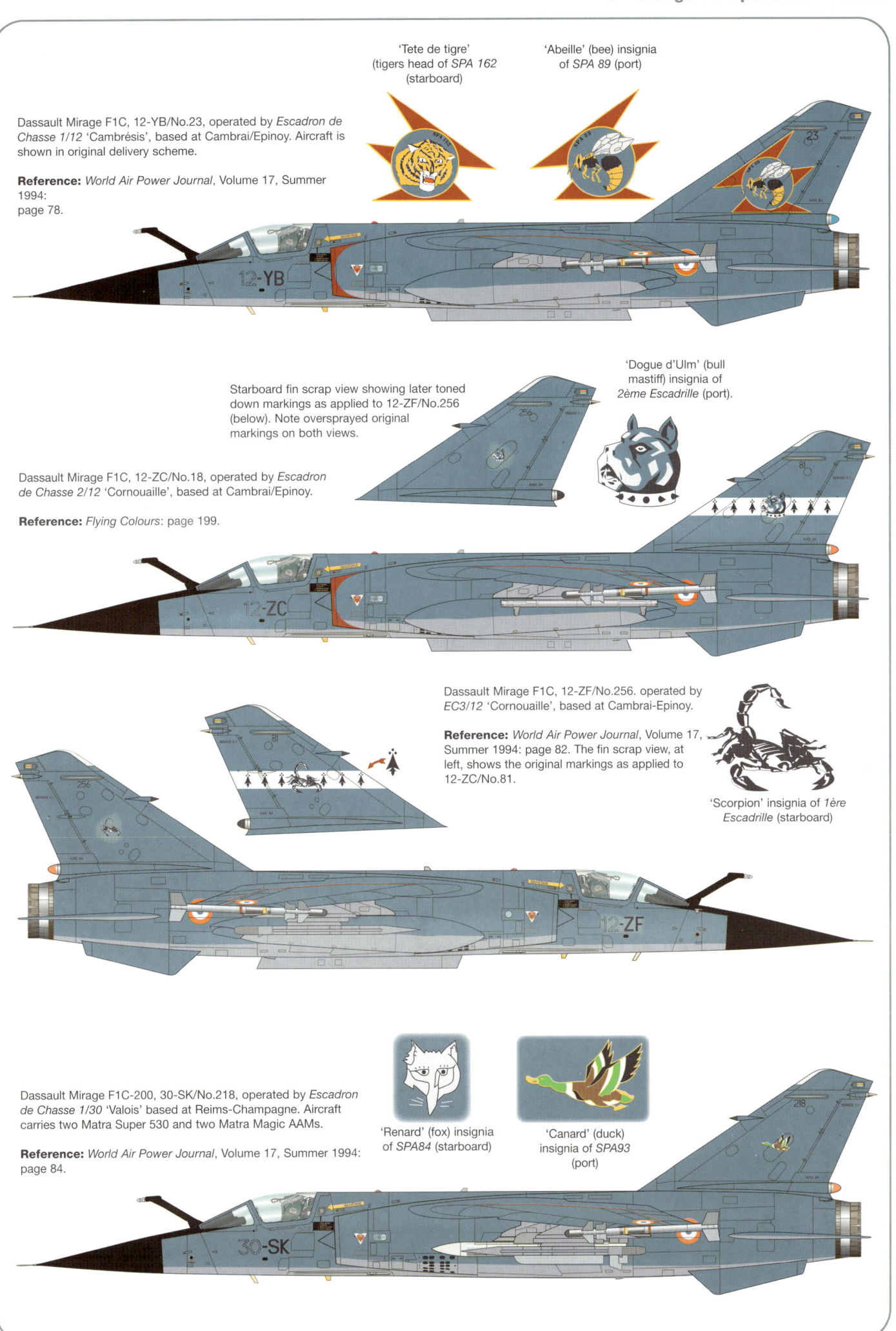

1 Mirage F1 Operators – France

this aircraft met most of the requirements of the *Armée de l'Air* and it was rapidly adopted as the new French multi-mission fighter aircraft, known as the Mirage F1. The private-venture design, which began as the Mirage III-E2 in mid-1964 and later known as III-F1, already bore the inscription 'Mirage F1C' when it conducted its maiden flight in December 1966. The following year was to prove eventful in the evolution of the design with the announcement, in January, that the *Armée de l'Air* had a possible requirement for one hundred Mirage F1s to plug a gap in its interceptor force. This was shortly followed by the loss of the Mirage F1 prototype just prior to the Paris Air Show. Any doubts about the future of the project were, however, allayed with the June announcement of France's withdrawal from the AFVG programme, which effectively signalled the official adoption of the Mirage F1. After the completion of '02', the first officially-sponsored aircraft at St. Cloud, it was transferred to Istres for its first flight on 20 March 1969. Following the completion of three development aircraft, a comprehensive test programme was conducted over the following two years. Aircraft '04', built to full production standards, joined the test programme in June 1970.

In spite of its commitment to a sizeable re-equipment programme for the *Armée de l'Air* during the 1970s, Dassault continued to pursue previous overseas operators of Mirage IIIs and potential new customers for the new multi-role fighter aircraft. Following one or two export successes, including Greece and South Africa, the company made strenuous efforts to secure the so-called 'Sale of the Century' involving the re-equipment of a number of NATO countries, including Belgium, Denmark, the Netherlands and Norway, with a replacement programme for the Lockheed F-104 Starfighter. Taking on the might of General Dynamics and Northrop, Dassault met with little success. The Mirage F1 International, later known as the F1E, had been offered with the more powerful SNECMA M53 Super Atar engine but eventually lost out to the General Dynamics F-16 Fighting Falcon in a result that was, ironically, announced at the 1975 Paris Air Salon. Dassault had, without doubt, lost a major sale although the simplicity, ruggedness and reliability of its design made the aircraft a natural choice for many other air forces.

Throughout the second half of the seventies, in yet another ironic twist in the F1 story, Dassault took advantage of American intransigence over the sale of military hardware to certain nations, to actively market this attractive design. As a result of an effective sales campaign, and some operational success, Dassault announced an impressive succession of orders, mainly to Middle Eastern countries before the end of the decade and the aircraft eventually went on to serve with eleven countries.

Dassault Mirage F1B, 33-FH/No.517 attached to *EC3/30* 'Lorraine', based at Reims-Champagne. The aircraft is specially marked to commemorate the disbandment of the FAFL Association on 21 June 2002 at it's home base.

Reference: *Check List No.1, AMD-BA Mirage F1*, DTU: page 41.

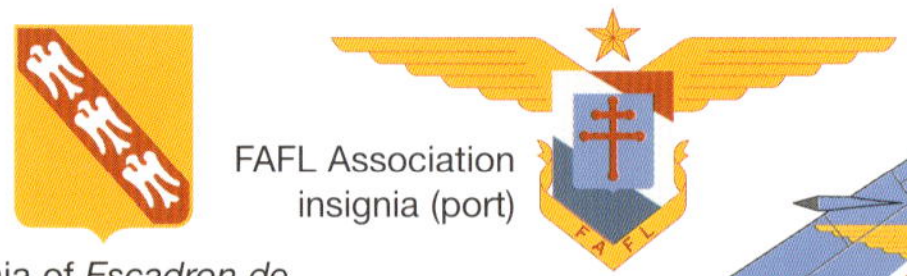

Insignia of *Escadron de Chasse 3/30* 'Lorraine' (starboard)

FAFL Association insignia (port)

Mirage F1 Operators – France

'Morietur' (morietur) insignia of *GC.II/9* (starboard)

'La Folie' (the jester) insignia of *SPA85* (port)

Dassault Mirage F1CT, 13-SA/No.245, operated by *Escadron de Chasse 3/13* 'Auvergne', based at Colmar-Mayenheim. Unit was renamed 'Alsace' in October 1993.

Reference: *World Air Power Journal*, Volume 17, Summer 1994: page 83.

'Chimère' (chimera) insignia of *SPA83* (starboard)

'Hirondelle' (sparrow) insignia of *SPA100* (port)

Dassault Mirage F1CT, 13-QE/No.280, operated by *Escadron de Chasse 1/13* 'Artois', based at Colmar-Meyenheim.

Reference: *Check List No.1, AMD-BA Mirage F1*, DTU: page 65.

CEAM insignia

Dassault Mirage F1B, 118-AT/No.512, operated by *Escadron de Chasse 24/118, Centre d'Expériences Aériennes Militaires (CEAM)*, based at Mont-de-Marsan, June 1986 Note that the aircraft carries the insignia of its previous unit, *1ère Escadrille ERC 571*, on the intake.

Reference: *Check List No.1, AMD-BA Mirage F1*, DTU: page 42.

'Fanion pirate' (pirate's pennant) insignia of *1ère Escadrille ERC 571*

Insignia of *Escadron de Chasse 5/330* 'Cote d'Argent'. Insignia known as 'The Office Clerk Tiger' (port side of fin)

Dassault Mirage F1C, 118-AK/No.2, operated by *Escadron de Chasse 24/118, Centre d'Expériences Aériennes Militaires (CEAM)*, based at Mont-de-Marsan. This is the second production F1 and carries high visibility markings for missile test photography.

Reference: *World Air Power Journal*, Volume 17, Summer 1994: page 87.

1 Mirage F1 Operators – France

By the beginning of the eighties, however, Dassault's attention had once again turned to marketing a new generation of delta-winged fighters in the shape of the Mirage 2000C and its derivatives and the emphasis shifted away from the Mirage F1. Production of new-build F1s quietly drew to a halt in 1991 by which time a total of 731 aircraft had been manufactured, including five prototypes and twenty embargoed Iraqi airframes. Although this final production figure may be less than Dassault's optimistic sales predictions of the early 1970s, it takes nothing away from the fact that the combat-proven Dassault Mirage F1 family of aircraft have served with an impressive number of air forces in a wide variety of roles and theatres with distinction over the last three decades.

France initially ordered thirty F1C interceptors in 1969 with further orders for fifty-five and twenty between 1971 and 1973 with the aim of acquiring 105 aircraft in-service by June 1977. The initial requirement was a Mach 2.5 capable high-altitude interceptor as a replacement for the Mirage IIIC force and possibly a fighter-bomber version to replace the Mirage IIIE. Since Dassault rarely built aircraft simply to meet *Armée de l'Air* requirements, the basic aircraft was offered in four sub-variants to attract export orders which included the Cyrano IV-radar equipped F1C and the multi-role F1E versions. Following a number of export successes and early operational experiences with the aircraft, particularly in South Africa, the *Armée de l'Air* saw the inherent versatility of the aircraft. Follow-on orders for the multi-role F1CR variant, to replace a variety of aircraft types, were placed in 1977, bringing production orders to 225 by 1980. These additional orders included, for the first time, the two-seat F1B operational trainer, the improved F1C-200 interceptor clearly identified by the fixed in-flight refuelling probe which also formed the basis for the single-seat export version, known as the F1E, and the F1CR reconnaissance variant. The two-seat F1B trainer retained the same operational equipment fit as the single-seat F1C although the internal 30 mm cannons were deleted. Following further trials with the *Centre d'Essais en Vol* (CEV – flight test centre) at Istres and the *Centre d'Expérimentaions Aériennes Militaires* (CEAM) at Mont-de-Marsan, the first production aircraft were joined by pilots and technicians from *Escadron de Chasse 30*, the premier French all-weather interceptor wing, for conversion work in the summer of 1973. *Escadron de Chasse Touts Temps (ECTT) 2/30*. 'Normandie-Niemen', based at Reims/Champagne were the first operational squadron to be re-equipped with the new fighter and were declared operational in December 1973, at which time they dropped the 'Touts Temps' designation and became *EC2/30*. By the following June, *EC3/30* 'Lorraine' had converted to the new type. The second wing, *EC5* at Orange/Caritat, started to convert to the Mirage F1C in August 1974, with both *EC1/5* 'Vendee' and *EC2/5* 'Ile de France' were declared operational by the end of the following year. *EC12* was the third wing to form at Cambrai/Epinoy in 1977 after *EC2/12* 'Cornouailles' started the process at Reims before relocating. *EC12* eventually became a three-Escadron Wing in 1980, following the re-establishment and redesignation of *EC2/12* 'Picardie', which joined *EC1/12* 'Cambresis' and the re-numbered *EC3/12* 'Cornouailles'. More squadrons followed including *EC3/5* 'Comtat Venaissin', which received all of the two-seat F1B aircraft and became the F1 OCU in 1981, and

A conventionally marked Mirage F1CR of *EC5/33* taxies out for another sortie during Exercise *Daring Eagle '02* at Beja, Southern Portugal.

This nice shot of Mirage F1CT (330-AJ/274) of *EC5/33* shows off the revised tactical wraparound camouflage scheme that underlines the primary strike attack mission of the aircraft. The dark green, as opposed to black nose radome, is also noteworthy in this view.

Mirage F1 Operators – France

EC1/10 'Valois' at Creil/Senlis. At the apogee of Mirage F1C/C-200 deployment with the *Armée de l'Air*, three and a half wings were equipped with the aircraft in the air-defence role. By 1982, nine out of the ten squadrons of *Commandement Air des Forces de Defense Aerienne* (*CAFDA*[1]) were equipped with the Dassault Mirage F1C/C-200. The Air Defence F1C/C-200 aircraft were delivered with medium grey-blue (*gris-bleu moyen*) uppersurfaces over matt silver undersides, with black radomes. Early, high-visibility unit and squadron markings were reduced in size from 1982 onwards as part of an overall toning down process for the Mirage F1 force. The first F1Cs to enter service did not have the Thomson-CSF BF Radar Warning Receivers fitted and possess 'clean' fins. Later F1Cs (from c/n 79 onwards) and all F1Bs, F1C-200s and F1CRs have fore- and aft-facing bullet fairings for the BF RWR. The F1C/C-200 was equipped with the Cyrano IV radar with air-to-air modes. Weapons, optimised for the principal air-defence role, included the BVR MATRA Super 530F AAM, two of which could be carried on underwing pylons and a pair of R550 Magic II IR-homing AAMs, mounted on wingtip rails. The aircraft also had two internally fitted 30 mm DEFA cannons.

Following a series of defence cuts, Creil closed as a permanent flying station in 1985 and the Mirage F1s of *EC1/10* were transferred to Reims, where they became the third squadron of *EC30*, as *EC3/30* 'Valois'. *EC4/30*, which had been based at Djibouti since 1979, was the last squadron to be re-equipped with the Mirage F1C. The unit converted from the Mirage III to the F1C in June 1988, when the first of eight aircraft arrived from France with a newly applied sand and dark chocolate colour scheme optimised for operations over the African landscape. *EC3/5*, the Mirage F1 OCU, became a regular air-defence squadron in the same year, in spite of the fact that other squadrons were starting to convert to the Mirage 2000C and some F1C-200s were being returned to the manufacturers for reworking as F1CTs. The OCU role then passed to a re-designated *EC3/30* 'Lorraine' at Reims. *EC3/5* operated the F1C-200 until 1990. Within five years, all but one of the air-defence squadrons equipped with the Mirage F1C/C-200 had re-equipped with the new delta-wing fighter or had been disbanded. *EC3/12* was destined to become the last squadron to operate the Mirage F1 in the air-defence role, when it disbanded in July 1995.

In the meantime, a further order for twenty-one aircraft had been placed during 1982 bringing the *Armée de l'Air* in-service figure to over 240 aircraft. In the same year, the *Armée de l'Air* started to take delivery of its final F1 variant from the initial orders, the F1CR, optimised for tactical reconnaissance. Many had favoured a version of the SEPECAT Jaguar for the tactical reconnaissance role but its half-British origin and a shortage of available airframes counted against the aircraft and the decision was taken to produce a reconnaissance version of the all-French Mirage F1. The prototype F1CRs were converted from F1C-200s taken from the Bordeaux production line and therefore possessed the stretched forward fuselage, fixed IFR probe and the Cyrano IVM radar with expanded air-to-ground capabilities. Unlike previous French tactical reconnaissance aircraft, such as the Mirage IIIR, which had been retro-fitted with dramatically re-designed nose sections to house the specialist role equipment role, the Mirage F1CR has a relatively limited internal mission fit with most of the new equipment carried in external, pylon mounted pods. This equipment included the RP-35P photo pod, which carries two 600 mm Omera 31 cameras for reconnaissance at medium- and high-level. Apart from its initial grey/green disruptive camouflage colour scheme over silver undersurfaces, externally, the F1CR looked almost identical to the original F1C-200 aircraft. The new version did introduce a distinctive undernose bulge with a lateral 'letterbox' aperture which was the access hatch for a camera bay housing Thomson-TRT (Omera) panoramic cameras. The starboard cannon was also deleted and replaced by a SAT SCM2400 Super Cyclope IRLS. Internally, the Mirage F1CR had a multi-role avionics suite, SAGEM Uliss 47 INS, a new Thomson-CSF VE-120 CRT HUD and refined cockpit displays. The F1CR was also fitted with the zero-zero SEM/Martin Baker Mk.10 ejection seat in place of the original, and less capable, F1RM4 seat fitted to most F1s. *ER2/33* 'Savoie' at Strasbourg/Entzheim took delivery of its first F1CR in June 1983 after which a second unit, *ER1/33* 'Belfort', began to re-equip from the Mirage IIIRD. A third unit *ER3/33* 'Moselle' was re-equipped in 1987.

From 1985 onwards, the Mirage F1CR was also operated by EC4/30 at the airport of Djibouti-Ambouli on the African Red Sea coast and aircraft assigned to that unit received the sand and dark chocolate camouflage scheme synonymous with that theatre of operations. In *Armée de l'Air* service, the Mirage F1CR is very much a multi-role aircraft, in spite of the apparent emphasis on its armed reconnaissance capabilities. As described later on, this particular variant also has an extremely effective secondary ground attack capability, which was frequently utilised during its early years in service. This capability was

[1] (Air Defence Forces Air Headquarters)

Mirage F1CT (30-QA/27) of *EC1/30* 'Alsace' at Colmar/Meyenheim photographed at RAF Fairford shortly after the end of the 1999 Kosovo campaign in which this particular aircraft took part. The aircraft carried a representative weapons load including the massive 2200 litre centreline drop tank. Note also the mission markings applied just below the cockpit canopy.

enhanced by the upgrade of the radar to Cyrano IVMR (*Modernisée Reconnaissance*) standards, which included the addition of ground and contour mapping and blind penetration modes. In spite of this, the aircraft was initially unable to employ precision laser-guided munitions. In 1999, some aircraft were retrofitted with the Thomson-CSF/Optronique ATLIS laser designator in place of the remaining DEFA cannon and the entire fleet also started to receive Corail flare dispensers attached to the root of the wing's lower surfaces. Some of the externally mounted mission equipment has also been upgraded, including the RAPHAEL SLAR pods. In July 1993, *ER3/33* 'Moselle' was disbanded and the two remaining squadrons of *ER33* left Strasbourg for their new home at Reims in April 1994. Since this time, Reims has hosted three F1 squadrons and supported a fourth detachment. Until recently, the base housed two F1CR squadrons, *EC1/33* 'Belfort' and *EC2/33* 'Savoie', together with the F1 Operational Conversion Unit, EC3/33 'Lorraine'. *EC3/33* operated a mixture of F1C single-seat and F1B twin-seat trainers but the squadron has since been disbanded, passing its aircraft to Colmar where the F1B trainers have been absorbed into an enlarged *EC1/30*, now the Mirage F1 OCU, and its F1CTs to both *EC1/30* and *EC2/30*. At the same time, the very last of the 'baseline' F1Cs were finally withdrawn from service. The fourth unit, the re-designated *EC4/33* 'Vexin' stationed in Djibouti, was destined to be the last operational F1C squadron in the *Armée de l'Air*, operating the type until August 2002. In 1999, the Mirage F1CR was upgraded to 'standard 6', which included the installation of GPS. The 'standard 7' upgrade, started in 2003, includes the installation of the 'Aigle' threat detector, which is far superior to the previously fitted 'SERVAL' system.

Although the Dassault Mirage 2000C had largely replaced the Mirage F1C-200s in the air-defence role towards the end of the 1980s, the *Armée de l'Air* could still see potential in the older aircraft, which spawned another fighter-bomber variant. In December 1988, with Mirage 2000C RDI deliveries well advanced, the *Armée de l'Air* embarked on a programme to convert forty-one surplus F1C-200 aircraft, with IFR capability to F1CT fighter-bombers to replace the ageing Mirage 5F derivative of the Mirage III. Dassault had originally built almost 200 Mirage F1C/C-200s for the *Armée de l'Air*. Although some of these so-called 'baseline' aircraft were retained in the air-defence and training role, it allowed the number of F1CT conversions to rise to a total of fifty-five in 1992. The new fighter-bomber variant was in many respects similar to the F1CR, but introduced a range of new avionics suites and a TMV 630A laser rangefinder in a new undernose fairing. The aircraft also received a new defensive aids suite, with Sherloc RHAWS. This equipment was housed in rectangular antenna fairings on the fin, providing the new variant with another recognition feature. The new avionics systems also necessitated the removal of the port DEFA cannon on this aircraft. The former air-defence fighters also lost their 'Mirage Bleu' colour scheme which gave way to a new tactical two-tone green/grey colour scheme, similar to that worn by the F1CR but extending to the undersurfaces. Some aircraft also received green nose radomes.

In spite of the emphasis on improved air-to-ground attack capabilities for the F1CT, the aircraft retained its original Cyrano IVM radar and the ability to carry both the MATRA Super 530F for air interception and R550 Magic II AAMs. As a result, front-line Mirage F1CTs often flew air-defence missions in support of the Mirage 2000C force until they lost this role in 1997, following the withdrawal of the Matra Super 530s. Since the strike and ground-attack roles remain the aircrafts' main forté, the air-to-ground weapon options cleared for use on the Mirage F1CT are extensive. They include GBU-12 Paveway II or French 400 or 1000 kg Laser Guided Bombs, BAP 100 runway denial weapons, BAT 120s, Belouga CBUs and MATRA F4 68 mm rocket pods. Externally carried mission support equipment for the F1CT includes Phimat chaff dispensers, Barax or the later Barracuda jamming pods and the aforementioned Corail flare dispensers. Following acceptance trials during 1992, the first operational unit to receive the F1CT was *EC1/13* 'Artois' at Colmar in November of that year. *EC3/13* 'Auvergne' received its first aircraft in April 1993 but both units time with the aircraft was short lived. In August 1993, the units became *EC1/13* 'Normandie-Neimen' and *EC3/13* 'Alsace' respectively, and the planned re-equipment of a third F1CT squadron was cancelled as the *Armée de l'Air* simultaneously adopted a new unit structure. Two years later the two F1CT units were re-designated again, retaining their titles but being renumbered *EC1/30* and *EC3/30* respectively.

All single-seat *Armée de l'Air* Mirage F1 variants have seen extensive operational use in over thirty years of service. In addition to those operational deployments that subsequently involved actual combat, described in more detail in Chapter 2, *Armée de l'Air* Mirage F1s have also seen widespread service elsewhere. Following their active participation in Operations *Manta* and *Epervier* during the 1980s, supporting the Chad army against Libya, Mirage F1s of the *Armée de l'Air* have continued to contribute to France's presence in this strategically important region. The Central African Republic remains a very important platform for French military operations in the region and the base at M'Poko, at Bangui's International Airport, is the second-largest *Armée de l'Air* installation in Africa. Since 1996, the Mirage F1CT has replaced the long-standing Jaguar detachment. *Detachment 7/33*, as it is known, consists of four Mirage F1CTs and two F1CRs from the parent *EC30* and *ER33* wings, respectively. On regular occasions, these aircraft have been called upon to maintain an active air presence in the often volatile region, including air power demonstrations over rebel bases. The largest *Armée de l'Air* detachment in Africa is currently maintained in Djibouti and the Mirage F1 was a key component of France's presence in this North East African state for more than fifteen years. As previously mentioned, *EC4/33* was the last unit to convert to the Mirage F1C and became the last operational squadron on the type when it was re-equipped with Mirage 2000s in 2002.

Soon after the end of air campaign that formed part of Operation *Desert Storm* (known as Operation *Daguet* in French parlance) in 1991, the Mirage F1CRs were called into action again during Operation *Aconit*, as part of Operation *Provide Comfort*, protecting the Kurdish people in northern Iraq before a long-term commitment to Operation *Northern Watch*, flying from Incirlik in Turkey. Four Mirage F1CRs deployed to Turkey in late July 1991 and were later joined by another four, which enabled the *Armée de l'Air* to conduct four sorties a day over northern Iraq. This detachment, maintained by the three component squadrons of *ER33* continued until 1996. The Mirage F1CRs were also based at Al Kharj in Saudi Arabia for some years on missions associated with Operation *Southern Watch* but were withdrawn prior to the last conflict with Iraq in 2003.

After almost eight years of deployment to the Balkans region in support of UN, and later NATO-sponsored operations over the states of the former Yugoslavia, *Armée de l'Air* Mirage F1s have returned to operating from their home bases. Success in these most recent air campaigns and ongoing investment in their equipment and tactics has confirmed the continued utility of this strike-attack and tactical reconnaissance aircraft in the current *Armée de l'Air* inventory. The four surviving Mirage F1CR/CT squadrons are now expected to remain in service for at least another five years whilst the F1CR, in particular, may actually soldier on until 2015 before being replaced by the Dassault Rafale.

Mirage F1 Operators – France

Dassault Mirage F1CR, 33-TA/No.661, operated by *ER3/33* 'Moselle'. The aircraft was finished in a special scheme for the *Red Flag* exercises held between 1987 and 1990. Other aircraft finished in such a way were 33-NK/609, 33-TR/653, 33-CC/648 and 33-TG/659.

Reference: *Check List No.1, AMD-BA Mirage F1*, DTU: page 50. Additional reference supplied by Marc Brouyere.

1 Mirage F1 Operators – France

This Mirage F1C (33-FK/52) of *EC3/33* 'Lorraine' at Reims/Champagne was one of two aircraft to attend the 1998 Royal International Air Tattoo at RAF Fairford. Unlike the other two Escadrons at Reims, that operate the upgraded F1CR variant, *EC3/33* still operate the baseline variant of the F1C seen here.

A very clean looking two-seat Mirage F1B operational trainer (33-FH/516) of *EC3/33*. This aircraft is unusual in that it has an in-flight refuelling probe fitted, a sight not often seen on the trainer variant in *Armée de l'Air* service.

Dassault Mirage F1C 32/33-FJ of *EC.3/33* 'Lorraine' in the standard *Armée de l'Air* Blue-Grey/Silver Air Defence scheme. Note the plain fin and small unit badge on the fin. (Photo: Lindsay Peacock)

Dassault Mirage F1C 83/33-FO of *EC3/33* 'Lorraine' wearing the sand coloured camouflage scheme associated with operations in Africa. The rather tatty appearance would suggest that this particular aircraft has just returned from theatre for a major overhaul at its Main Operating Base. (Photo: Lindsay Peacock)

Two views of a rather smart looking Dassault Mirage F1C (c/n 87/30-ST), which contrast nicely with the previous photograph. This aircraft, photographed at Reims in 1993, wears a very clean looking sand and brown camouflage scheme with standard national markings but no unit markings, which would indicate that it has just been prepared for deployment to Central Africa or Djibouti. (Photo: Lindsay Peacock)

1 Mirage F1 Operators – Morocco/Libya

Royal Moroccan Air Force *(Al Quwwat al Jawwiya al Malakiya Marakishiya)*

France's close relationship with Morocco resulted in a substantial order for the Mirage F1 from this North African nation in December 1975. A total of forty-five aircraft were eventually ordered and delivered including twenty-five F1CH interceptors, fourteen F1EH and six F1EH-200 multi-role fighters, the latter equipped with in-flight refuelling probes.

All of the aircraft were fitted with BF radar warning receivers and VOR aerials. Later, flare dispensers were fitted to the rear fuselage above the ventral fins and an ECM pod to one of the wingtips. Other modifications to Moroccan F1s included RP35 underwing drop tanks fitted with grenade launchers and an indigenously produced centreline reconnaissance pod, jointly developed by Aero Maroc Industries in collaboration with Dassault. Air-defence weapons include the MATRA R.530 and 550 Magic 1R AAMs. Initial deliveries of Mirage F1 were expedited by France with the transfer of aircraft destined for the *Armée de l'Air*, following Moroccan intervention in a little publicised conflict with Algerian and Libyan-backed *Polisario* guerrillas in the Western Sahara (see Chapter 2). During the 1990s, severe financial restrictions thwarted Morocco's attempts to acquire more modern combat aircraft so its remaining fleet of Mirage F1s underwent an upgrade programme with Dassault in 1996/97. At least two, and possibly three, squadrons still operate the surviving Mirage F1CH/EH aircraft from Sidi Slimane AB. These aircraft regularly participate in air exercises, providing 'opposition' to international visitors, including US Navy Carrier Air Groups, taking advantage of Morocco's excellent low-flying training facilities. The Moroccan Mirages have also become increasingly involved in overseas deployments, particularly to France, for joint exercises.

Moroccan Air Force Dassault Mirage F1CH (c/n 127) on finals during a Joint Air Exercise in France. This well maintained aircraft is shown in a 'clean' configuration with the exception of the centreline mounted drop tank. Note also the chaff/flare dispenser fitted above the ventral strake, which appears to be similar to those fitted to Spanish F1Ms. (Photo Emiel Bonte)

Libyan Arab Republic Air Force

Libya was another early customer for the F1, ordering a total of thirty-eight in 1974. The order included sixteen each of the F1ED and F1AD single-seat fighters and six F1BD two-seat trainers. As previously mentioned, Libya was one of only two customers to order and operate the ground-attack F1A variant. These aircraft were delivered between January and April 1978 to the 1011th Fighter Squadron based at Okhba Ibn-Nafi AB near Tripoli. The two-seat F1BD trainers were subsequently delivered to the same unit between April 1978 and October 1979. The sixteen Mirage F1ED interceptors, equipped with the Cyrano IV-I radar and armed with MATRA R.530 and Magic air-to-air missiles, were delivered to the 1012th Fighter Squadron at the same air base between January 1978 and October 1979. It is understood that some of the aircraft were re-deployed to the south of the country for operations over the disputed territories of Chad, where French intervention risked the prospect for F1 versus F1 aerial combat, which never materialised (see Chapter 2). The 1012th Fighter Squadron was very active during regular encounters with US Navy fighters from the Mediterranean-based Sixth Fleet during the early to mid-1980s, but the subsequent suspension of French technical support caused a number of difficulties, particularly with the maintenance of the Cyrano IV-I radars which rendered the Matra R.530FE medium-range missile systems useless. It is believed that at least some of the Mirage F1s redeployed to Gamal Abdul Nasser airfield (formerly RAF El Adem) outside Tobruk, from where they regularly 'buzzed' American fleet aircraft carriers. In fact, two Libyan Mirage F1s encountered USN F-14A Tomcats from *USS Nimitz* in August 1981 the day before a pair of American aircraft from VF-41 destroyed two Libyan Su-22 'Fitters' in a brief air-to-air engagement over the Gulf of Sidra. Although long-term sanctions against Libya, which has resulted in the intermittent overhaul of their Mirage F1 fleet, means that their current status is unknown, unconfirmed reports suggest that both the 1011th and 1012th Fighter Squadrons remains operational with at least a dozen Mirage F1ADs and eight or nine F1EDs, respectively.

1 Mirage F1 Operators – Morocco

Dassault Mirage F1CH, No.152, operated by the 'Assad' Squadron, Moroccan Air Force (*Al Quwwat al Jawwiya al Malakiya Marakishiya*), based at Sidi Slimane. Aircraft carries two Matra Magic R550 air-to-air missiles on wingtip launch rails, and one Matra 530 semi-active radar-homing missile on the centreline.

Reference: *Check List No.1, AMD-BA Mirage F1*, DTU: page 108 (third photograph from top).

Dassault Mirage F1EH-1-200, No.172, operated by the 'Atlas' Squadron, Moroccan Air Force (*Al Quwwat al Jawwiya al Malakiya Marakishiya*), based at Sidi Slimane. The aircraft carries two Matra Magic R550 air-to-air missiles, and an indigenous Aero Maroc reconnaissance pod on the aircraft centreline.

Reference: *Check List No.1, AMD-BA Mirage F1*, DTU: page 108.

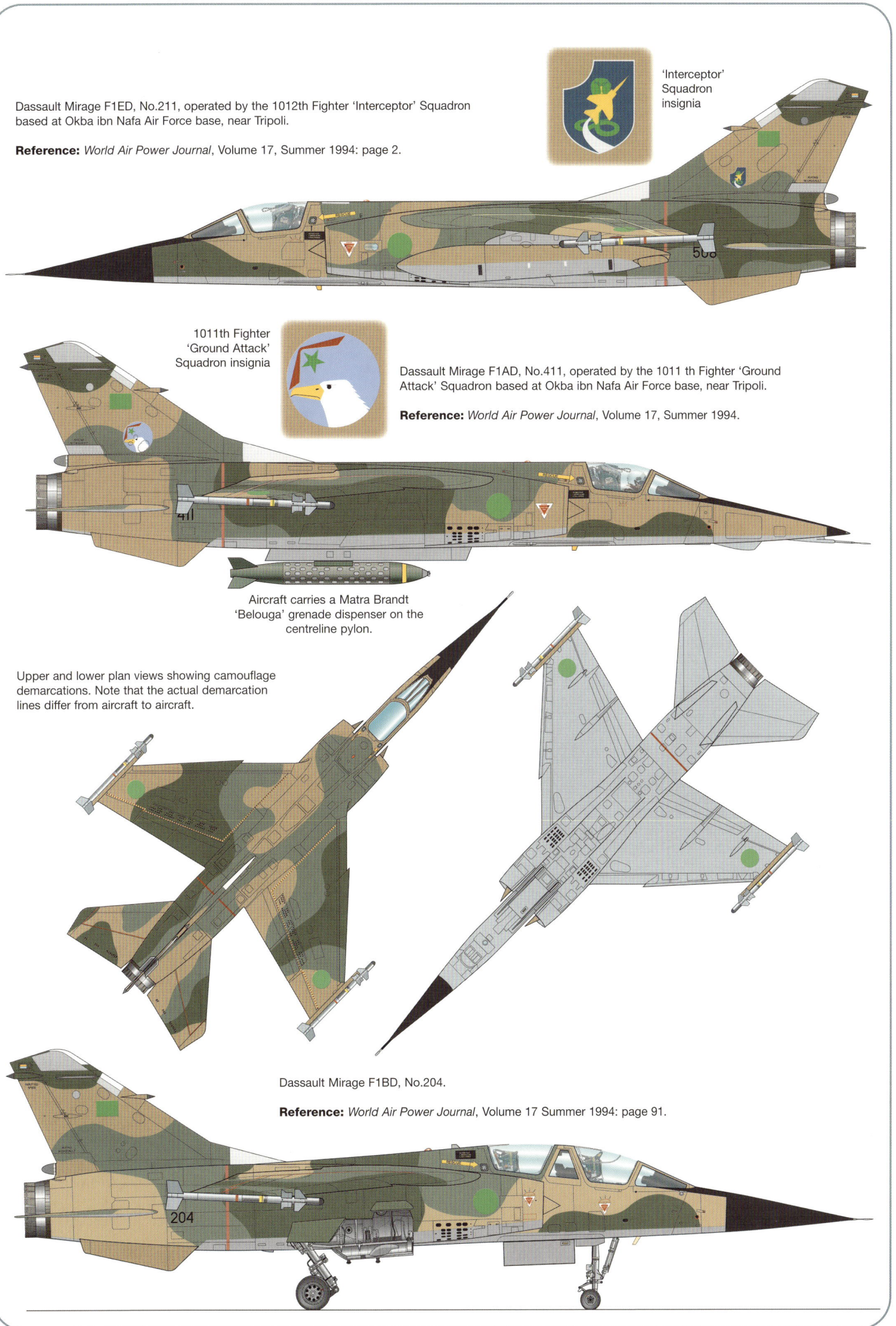

South African Air Force *(Suid-Afrikaanse Lugmag)*

South Africa's somewhat clandestine announcement of an order for the new Dassault Mirage F1 fighter did not initially reveal the fact that the South African Air Force was the first of only two air forces to order the non-radar ground-attack optimised Mirage F1A variant. A first order, for sixteen F1CZ interceptors, was placed in 1974 and the aircraft were handed over between September of that year and July 1975. The first aircraft to be delivered to South Africa was flown in April 1975 and following the local license-manufacture of the majority of the order, No.3 Squadron was formed on the new type at Waterkloof AB near Pretoria. A second, larger, order was subsequently placed for the F1AZ, a simpler and cheaper variant, equipped with an alternate EMD AIDA 2 target ranging radar optimised for ground-attack. The first aircraft in this series flew in March 1976 and a total of thirty-two aircraft equipped a single unit (No.1 Squadron) at Waterkloof, making this the largest unit in the service. The aircraft were all fitted with BF radar warning receivers and VOR aerials as standard with the F1AZ featuring a laser rangefinder and Aida II ranging radar in a small nose radome. All the aircraft initially wore a distinctive camouflage scheme of olive drab and deep buff over light grey undersurfaces. Weapons initially supplied to South Africa included the long-range MATRA R.530ZE and 550 Magic 1 AAMs for air-defence and MATRA F.4 rocket pods and Mk.82 bombs for ground-attack. Concerns about France joining the UN arms embargo led South Africa's Armaments Development and Production Corporation (Armscor) to begin Research and Development into indigenous weapons systems and the Armscor V3 Kukri, externally identical to the MATRA Magic AAM, and a developed version known as the Armscor Darter subsequently equipped the F1CZ force. Locally-produced ground-attack weapons and CFD-200 chaff/flare dispensers were also employed by the F1AZ force in order to guarantee continued operational effectiveness for the increasingly isolated SAAF. Both Mirage F1 squadrons were part of Strike Command until this formation became Air Defence Command in January 1980. In 1981, No.1 Squadron relocated to Hoedspruit AB while the Mirage F1CZs of No.3 Squadron remained at Waterkloof for their entire career. Both variants served with distinction in the SAAF and were at the forefront of air operations into Angola and anti-guerrilla strikes into the administered territory of South-West Africa (now known as Namibia) during the long 'Bush War' of the seventies and eighties (See Chapter 2). During this time, the SAAF Mirage F1 force conducted several trials with new camouflage schemes and eventually adopted two different, low-visibility schemes to reflect their air defence and ground attack roles. The cessation of hostilities with Angola and the change of administration in South Africa brought about fundamental changes to the size and structure of South Africa's armed forces and the SAAF were forced to disband No.3 Squadron as an economy measure in September 1992, although the F1AZs of No.1 Squadron continued in service until November 1997. During the twilight years of their service, and before the lifting of international sanctions against South Africa, two of the F1AZ variants were the subject of some highly complex indigenous modification programmes designed to expand the operational capability of this aircraft, both for the SAAF and other Mirage F1 customers. The first aircraft, Mirage F1AZ (c/n 235) received a highly sophisticated avionics fit and other improvements, including a comprehensive Defensive Aids Suite (DAS), the result of SAAF experience and research during the 'Bush War'. The aircraft, which wore a striking Dark/Light Blue and White colour scheme, was described locally as an 'Avionics Technology Demonstrator'. It became known, more affectionately, as 'The World's Fastest Dairy Truck' – a reference to the corporate colours of a major South African dairy producer – and received appropriate titles. Today, this unique aircraft is preserved in the SAAF Museum at Swartkop AB, where it was comprehensively photographed for this title (see Chapter 5). Even more impressive was an attempt by Aerosud, an indigenous engine manufacturer, to re-engine the SAAF F1 fleet with a modified Russian SMR-95 engine. Two engines were shipped to South Africa where the Atlas Aircraft Company planned to fit them in both the F1AZ and CZ variants. In April 1992, it was reported that a SAAF Mirage F1 fuselage was transported to Russia for similar trials. The SMR-95, a modified version of the RD-33 engine fitted to the MiG-29 'Fulcrum', was considerably lighter than the Atar engine and offered 10 per cent more thrust so the performance of the modified aircraft was keenly anticipated. The so-called Super-Mirage F1AZ (c/n 216) first flew with the new engine in 1994 and proved to be a highly manoeuvrable and effective aircraft, but further development work on behalf of the SAAF was curtailed following the lifting of international sanctions and the South African Government's desire to procure new generation aircraft types. The unmodified F1AZ fleet thus continued operating from Hoedspruit AFB for a further three years before the long and illustrious career of the Mirage F1 in SAAF service came to an end on 25 November 1997. The majority of F1AZs were subsequently placed into storage pending attempts to sell them on the international market. In an interesting footnote to the South African Mirage F1 story, Russian and South African aerospace companies entered into a partnership agreement and attempted to market the surplus Mirage F1 fleets. In 2001, Mirage F1AZ (c/n 216) was taken out of storage and shipped to Zhukovsky in an Ilyushin Il-76 where the airframe was re-united with the SMR-95 engine. The SAAF Mirage F1AZ flew again in this configuration on 9 August 2001 at Zhukovsky and became the first foreign military aircraft to participate in the Moscow International Aviation and Space Salon (MAKS) held at Zhukovsky a week later, providing a very impressive aerial demonstration in the hands of a SAAF pilot. The aircraft was actively marketed with the new engine and avionics and was reportedly capable of being equipped with four R-73E AA-11 'Archer' air-to-air missiles. To date, the project has met with little success with the majority of aircraft remaining in storage or on public display following donations to museums in South Africa. It has recently been reported that at least two ex-SAAF F1AZs have since been acquired by Gabon but their operational status was not known when this book went to press.

This SAAF Mirage F1AZ sports the three-tone low-visibility camouflage colour scheme with toned down national and unit markings, applied to the AZ fleet during the latter part of their service career. (Photo: Paul Dubois)

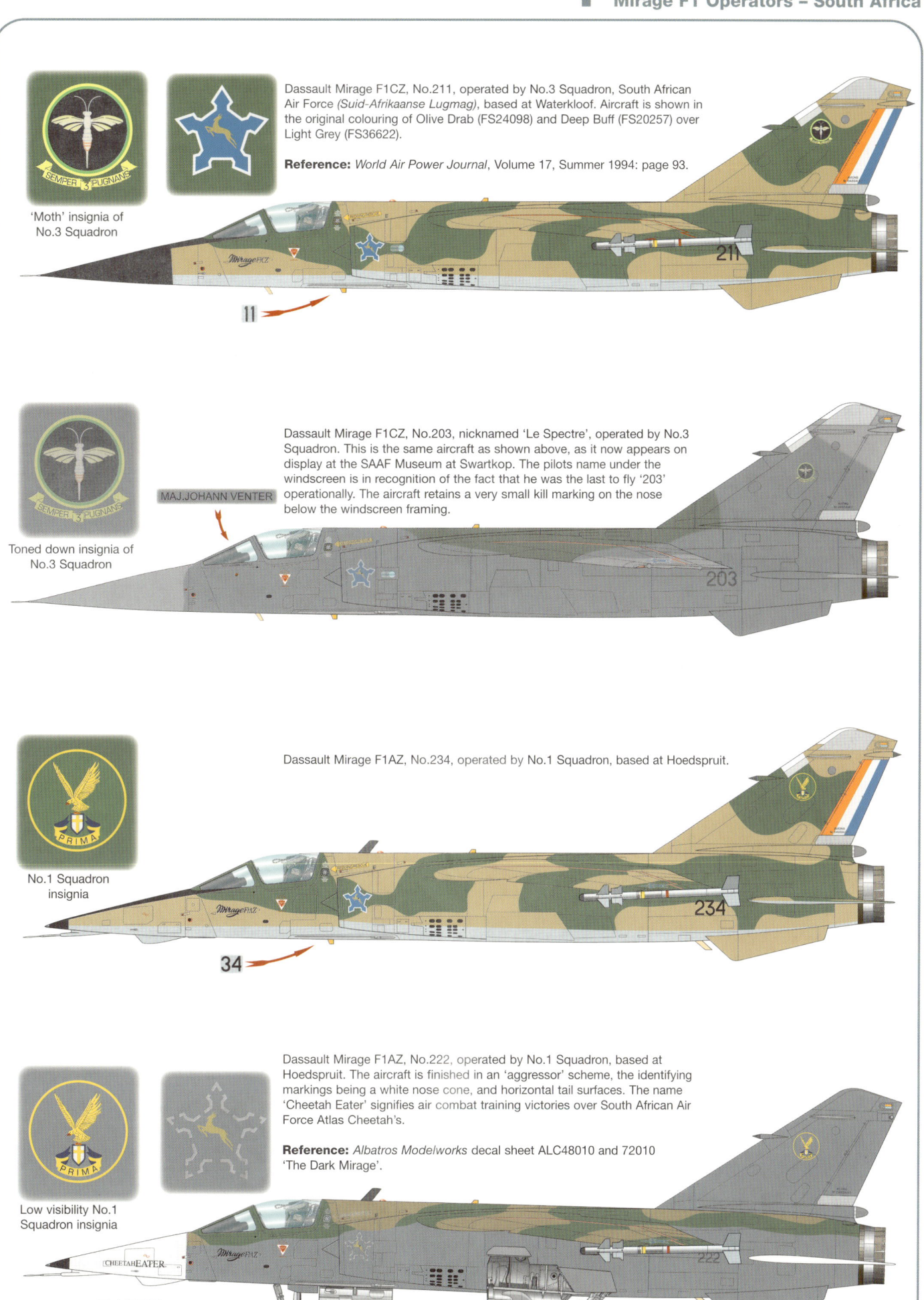

1 Mirage F1 Operators – Jordan

Royal Jordanian Air Force (Al Quwwat al Jawwiya al Malakiya al Urduniya)

Dassault benefited from further American intransigence over the supply of combat aircraft to Middle Eastern states when it picked up a Saudi Arabian initiated contract in mid-1979 to supply seventeen single-seat F1CJ interceptors and two twin-seat F1BJ aircraft to Jordan as replacements for Lockheed F-104A Starfighters. The first of these aircraft was delivered to Mont-de-Marsan for crew training in January 1981 before re-equipping No.25 Squadron at Shaheed Mwaffaq as-Salti AB. Saudi Arabia also funded the delivery of a further seventeen multi-role F1EJs, which were delivered between June 1982 and June 1983 and equipped No.1 Squadron. All three variants have BF radar warning receivers and VOR aerials fitted. The F1CJ and BJ aircraft sported a two-tone light-grey colour scheme, reflecting their air-defence mission while the multi-role F1EJs wore a three-tone camouflage scheme over light grey undersurfaces. Weapons supplied to Jordan included the MATRA Super 530F-1 and 550 Magic 1 AAMs for air-defence and laser-guided Aerospatiale AS30L air-to-surface missiles for precision attack. Plans to increase and upgrade the Jordanian Mirage F1 fleet were severely hampered by Jordan's support for Iraq during the Gulf War of 1991 and a withdrawal of Saudi Arabian funding. As a result, Jordan has been forced to reduce the number of aircraft in service and at present 1 Squadron are believed to be the sole operator of the type, flying a mix of all three variants.

A RJAF Dassault Mirage F1CJ, in near 'clean' condition with just two wingtip mounted Matra Magic missiles fitted, no doubt for an air-defence sortie. (Photo: Rogier Westerhuis)

Royal Jordanian Air Force Dassault Mirage F1EJ formats on a Northrop F-5A Freedom Fighter during a joint air exercise. The colour schemes on both of these aircraft show evidence of the harsh environment in which they operate. Note the replacement cockpit canopy on the Mirage F1EJ, which appears to have been 'robbed' from a F1CJ. (Photo: Rogier Westerhuis)

Dassault Mirage F1EJ of No.1 Squadron, taxies out from its revetment in the heat of midday. This particular aircraft is carrying a reconnaissance pod on the centreline pylon and a Thomson Barracuda self-defence pod on the port outboard weapons pylon. (Photo: Rogier Westerhuis)

1 Mirage F1 Operators – Jordan

Dassault Mirage F1CJ, No.2507, operated by No.25 Squadron, Royal Jordanian Air Force (*Al Quwwat al Jawwiya al Malakiya al Urduniya*), based at Shaheed Mwaffaq-as-Salti air base, Azraq, early 1980s.

Reference: *World Air Power Journal*, Volume 17, Summer 1994.

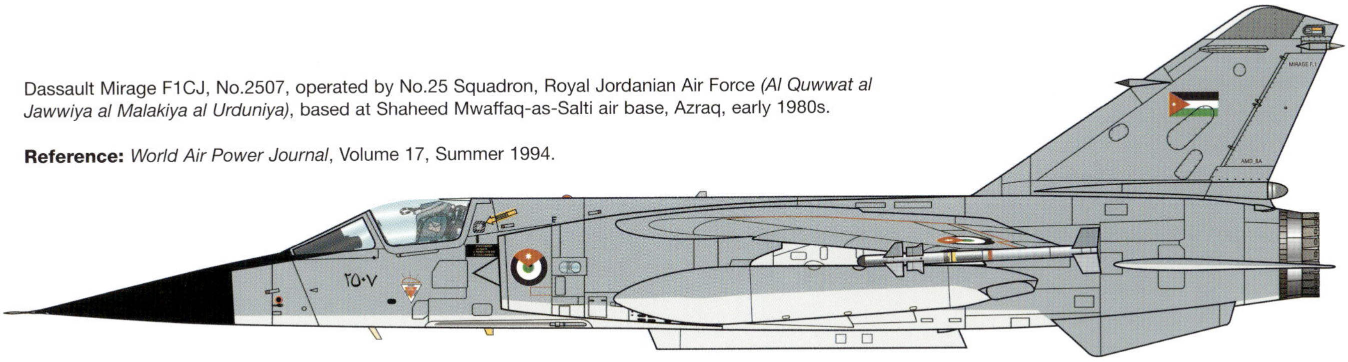

Upper and lower views – these are representative views for general camouflage layout. Camouflage demarcation differs from aircraft to aircraft.

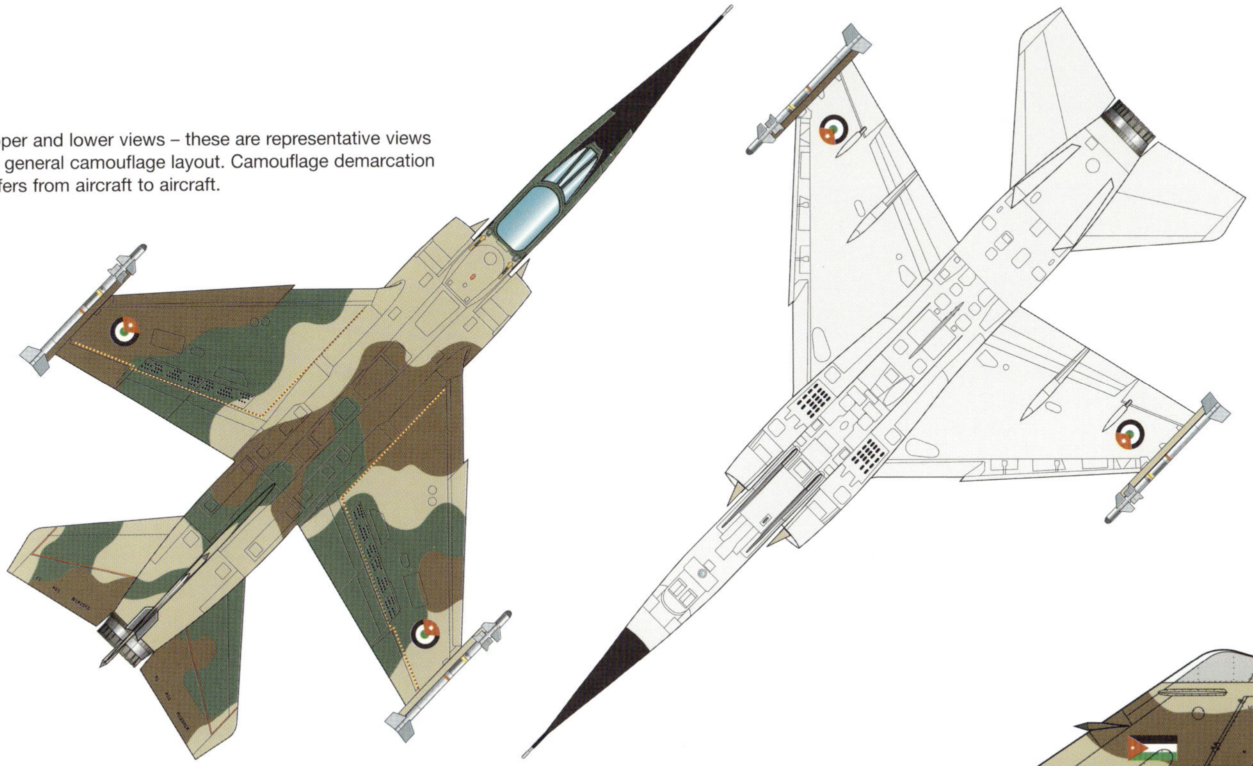

Dassault Mirage F1EJ, No.108, operated by No.1 Squadron, Royal Jordanian Air Force.

Reference: *World Air Power Journal*, Volume 17, summer 1994: page 90; *Arab Air Forces*, Squadron Signal Publications: page 33.

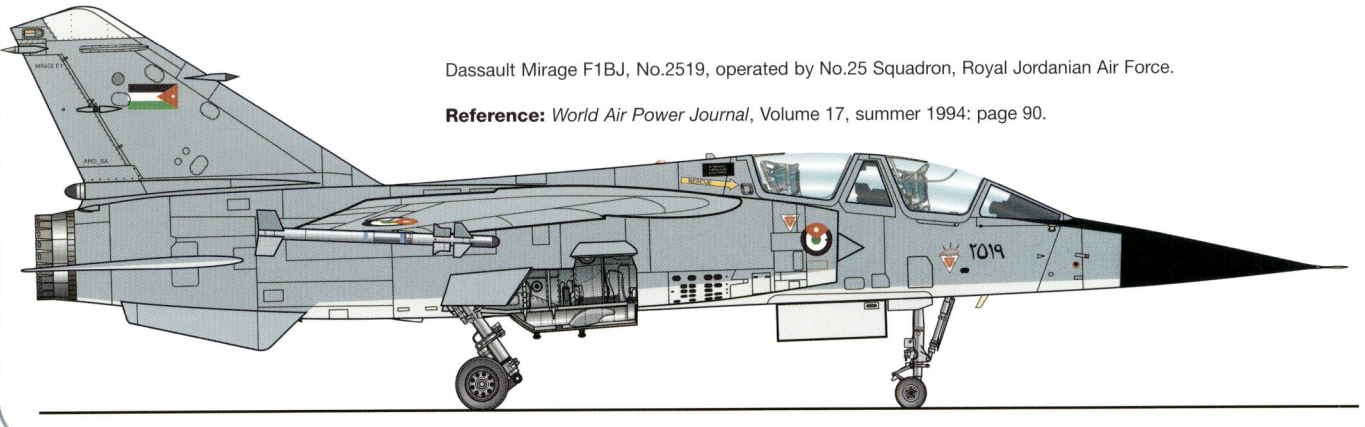

Dassault Mirage F1BJ, No.2519, operated by No.25 Squadron, Royal Jordanian Air Force.

Reference: *World Air Power Journal*, Volume 17, summer 1994: page 90.

17

Iraqi Air Force (Al Quwwait al Jawwiya al Iraquiya)

Another Middle East customer, Iraq, was to become the biggest overseas customer for the Mirage F1 with initial orders for thirty-six aircraft, and further options on another thirty-six, in June 1977. A total of eighteen F1EQ-1 and fourteen F1EQ-2 single-seat fighters plus four F1BQ-1 and -2 trainers and associated Super 530F-1 and Magic 1 AAMs were acquired with deliveries starting in April 1980. By this time, Iraq was engaged in its long eight-year war with Iran and envisaged the need for more aircraft, fulfilled when France declined to join the international arms embargo. Further orders for F1BQ-3 two-seat and F1EQ-4 single-seat aircraft, with an in-flight refuelling capability, were placed shortly afterwards and these were supplemented by further deliveries up until 1989. In all, Iraq ordered a total of 128 Mirage F1BQ and F1EQ aircraft although not all were delivered. All of the Iraqi aircraft had a distinctive HF fillet aerial in the leading edge join between the fin and fuselage together with BF radar warning receivers. VOR/ILS aerials were fitted to the majority of their aircraft. The first thirty-two F1EQ aircraft delivered were employed as interceptors and during the war with Iran claimed at least thirty-five aerial victories (see Chapter 2). Deliveries of the Mirage F1EQ-4, Iraq's first multi-role Mirage variant, commenced in December 1982 and mission equipment included the COR-2 reconnaissance pod. The F-1EQ-5s were fitted with the Thomson-CSF Agave radar in place of the standard Cyrano IV for their dedicated anti-shipping role with Aerospatiale Exocet missiles. The last few -5s were delivered with a blue-grey camouflage colour scheme in lieu of the standard Iraqi colour scheme of sand and chocolate over light grey undersurfaces. Further improvements resulted in the F1EQ-6 variant, of which eighteen were delivered, which had the BF RWR replaced by the Thomson-CSF SHERLOC system. By 1989, when Dassault terminated the delivery of further Mirage F1s as a result of non-payments, Iraq had received a total of ninrty-three single-seat F1EQs and fifteen two-seat F1BQ aircraft. The later -4, -5 and -6 versions were assigned to attack and reconnaissance missions using a variety of French supplied munitions including Aerospatiale AM39 Exocet, AS30L laser-guided missiles, MATRA ARMAT anti-radiation missiles and Thomson-Brandt 68 mm and 100 mm rockets. Later, after French sanctions on the supply of air delivered weapons were imposed, the Iraqi aircraft were reportedly modified to accept weapons of Soviet origin including the X29L (AS-14 'Kedge') air-to-surface missile. Iraqi Mirage F1s also took part in the so-called 'Tanker War' during their conflict with Iran (see Chapter 2). At least a dozen Mirage F1s were reported lost in action during the Iran-Iraq war although this figure is likely to be higher. By 1990, it is believed that fifteen single-seat F1EQs and F1EQ-2s, together with eleven of the two-seat F1BQs, remained, all based at Qayyarah West, Kut al Hayy East and Al Asad. The surviving F1EQ-4, -5 and -6 versions, all assigned to attack duties, were operating from Al Sahra, Qayyarah South, Tikrit an Talill. It has also been reported that Iraq and Jordan proposed a joint Mirage F1 squadron at H-3 airfield in 1990 to compensate for overall Iraqi losses, but this Unit did not form. Estimates suggest that Iraq fielded a total of sixty-two Mirage F1EQs and eleven F1BQs at the start of Operation *Desert Storm* in 1991. An Iraqi Mirage F1 was the first aircraft to be downed during the subsequent air campaign and further losses followed before twenty-four of the type took refuge in Iran where they continue to be impounded. Prior to the most recent Iraqi conflict, a small number of Mirage F1s were understood to be operational with either the 79th or 89th Fighter Squadron based at Qayyara. Like the rest of the Iraqi Air Force, they took no part in the defence of Iraq and their current status is still unclear.

Iraqi Air Force Dassault Mirage F1BQ two-seat conversion trainer (c/n 4504) during a stopover on its pre-delivery flight. Note the two-tone desert camouflage scheme, lack of national insignia, complete absence of wing pylons or stores and the in-flight refuelling probe. (Photo: Lindsay Peacock)

In contrast to the 'clean' two-seat F1BQ shown above, this Iraqi Air Force F.1Q (c/n 4501), photographed on the same pre-delivery flight, has a 'buddy' refuelling pod fitted to the fuselage centreline pylon and two silver-coloured drop tanks on underwing stores pylons. Note the IFR probe and the extended fin fillet on this particular variant. (Photo: Lindsay Peacock)

1 Mirage F1 Operators – Iraq

Dassault Mirage F1EQ-4-200, No.4526/Y-BLU, Iraqi Air Force *(Al Quwwat al Jawwiya al Iraqiya)*, shown in test and delivery scheme. Aircraft carries no national insignia, with call-sign carried on fin. Last two letters of call-sign are carried on intake. The aircraft is equipped with a large 2,200 litre 'Irakien' centreline tank used on ferry flights. As can be seen, ground clearance is minimal.

Reference: *Aerofax Minigraph 17, Dassault Mirage F1*, Aerofax Inc: page 23.

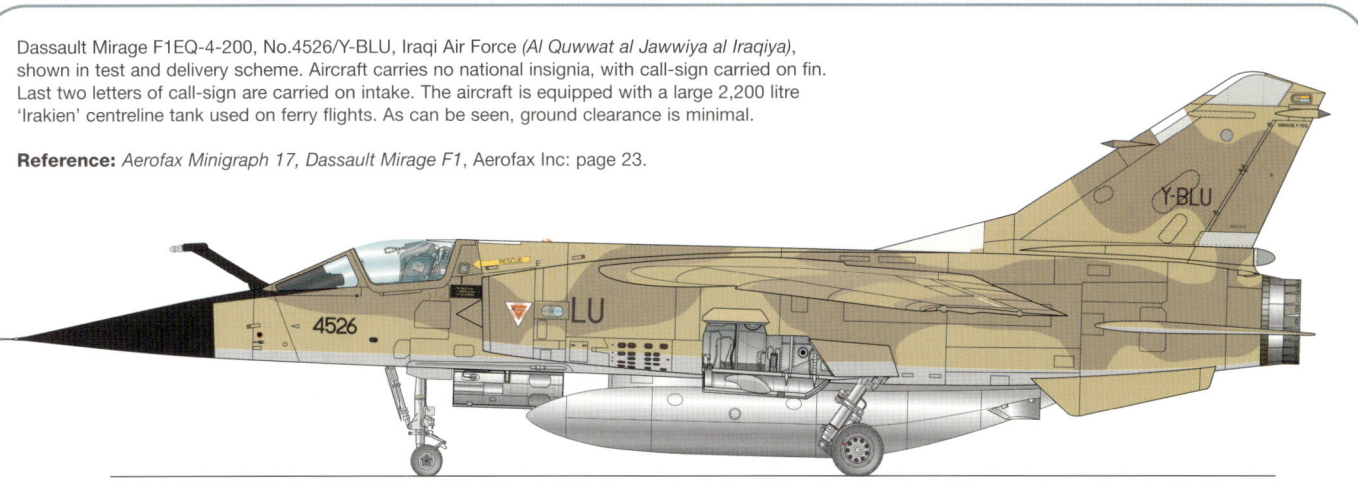

Dassault Mirage F1EQ, No.4010, 92nd Fighter Squadron, Iraqi Air Force *(Al Quwwat al Jawwiya al Iraqiya)*. Aircraft is shown in the standard scheme carried at the time of the Iran-Iraq war.

Reference: *World Air Power Journal*, Volume 17, Summer 1994: page 89.

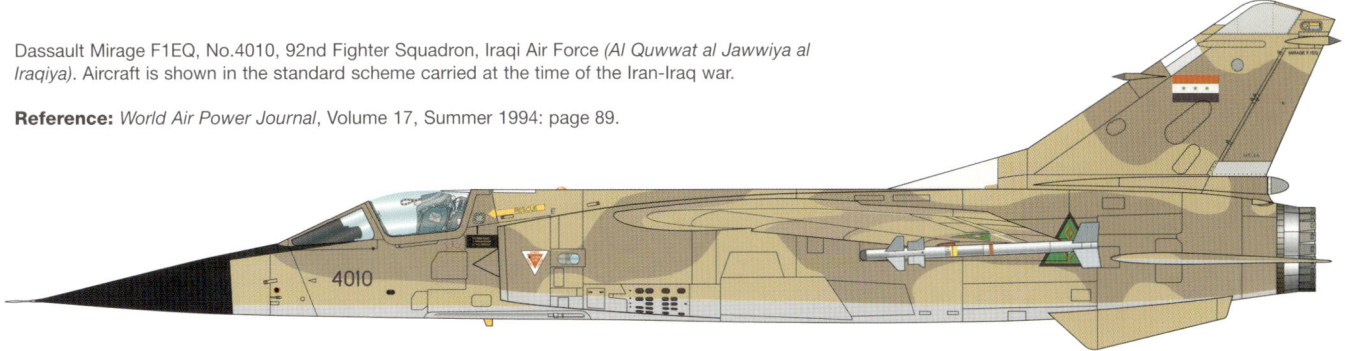

Dassault Mirage F1EQ-5-200, Iraqi Air Force *(Al Quwwat al Jawwiya al Iraqiya)*. The aircraft is finished in the later Slate Grey over Grey scheme adopted for over-water operations.

Reference: *World Air Power Journal*, Volume 17, Summer 1994: page 90.

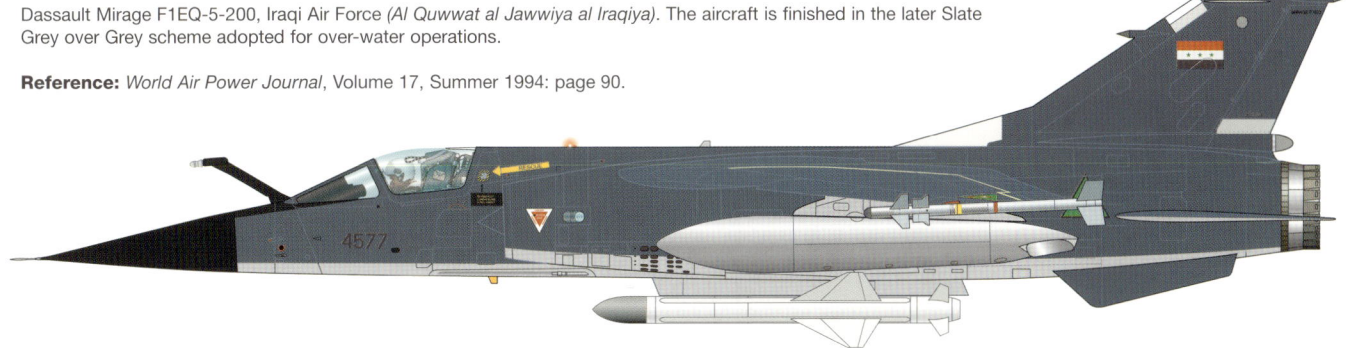

Dassault Mirage F1BQ, Iraqi Air Force *(Al Quwwat al Jawwiya al Iraqiya)*. Iraq used a total of fifteen two-seaters. Aircraft is equipped with two 1,200 litre drop tanks.

Reference: *World Air Power Journal*, Volume 17, Summer 1994: page 89.

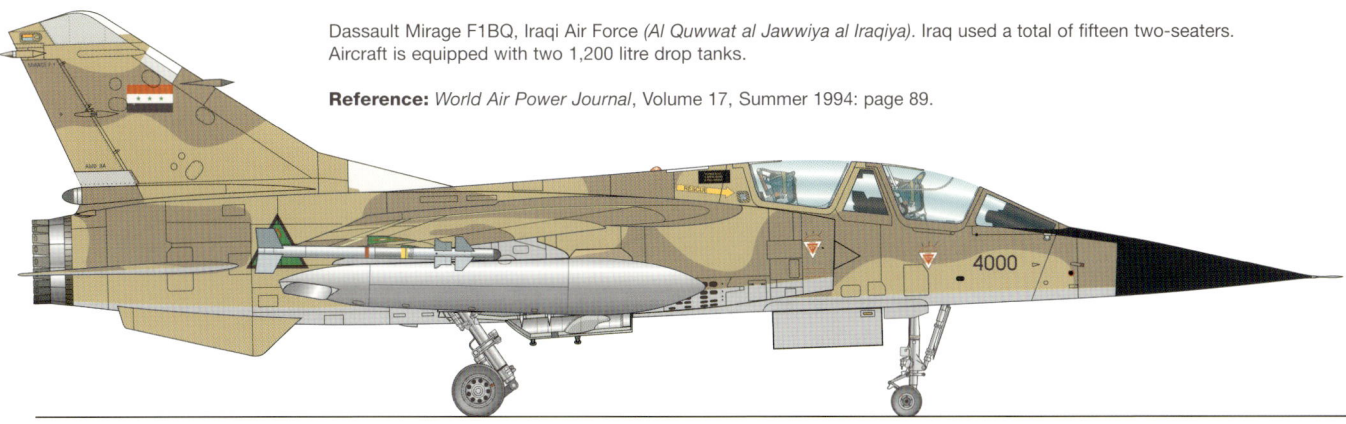

Kuwait Air Force (Al Quwwait al Jawiya al Kuwaitiya)

A long standing border dispute between Kuwait and Iraq, which resulted in clashes during 1973, prompted the former to acquire new aircraft to replace its BAC Lightnings which it had found too complex to operate. An original American offer of assistance with the supply of refurbished LTV F-8 Crusaders was turned down in favour of the new Mirage F1. Kuwait actually became the launch customer for the two-seat Mirage F1B ordering two F1BK trainers, to go with eighteen F1CK interceptors in April 1974. Initial deliveries took place between July 1976 and October 1977. A follow-on order for nine F1CK-2s and four F1BK-2s was announced in February 1983 to compensate for an abnormally high attrition rate. The F1CK and BK aircraft were delivered with VOR and BF radar warning receivers and sported a two-tone sand camouflage scheme over light grey undersurfaces. The later -2 aircraft were delivered in an overall two-tone grey colour scheme. In spite of their F1C designations, the newer aircraft were essentially F1E multi-role fighters and the earlier -1 aircraft were subsequently brought up to the same standard to provide commonality across the fleet. New armaments, including MATRA Super 530F-1 and ARMAT anti-radar missiles were procured in 1983 together with Thomson-CSF Remora jamming pods. The Mirage F1s eventually equipped two squadrons, 18 and 61, at Ali al Salem AB. Following the Iraqi invasion of Kuwait in 1990, and the loss of some aircraft to shelling, fifteen aircraft escaped to Taif in Saudi Arabia, subsequently re-grouping at Dhahran. Sporting newly-applied 'FREE KUWAIT' titles, the pilots trained for the liberation of their homeland whilst *Armée de l'Air* Mirage F1CR groundcrew, deployed for Operation *Trident*, the French contribution to Operation *Desert Storm*, provided technical support. The Kuwaiti Mirage F1 crews eventually completed 128 combat missions over their homeland during the conflict. Unconfirmed reports also suggest that between six to eight aircraft were taken back to Iraq in late 1990. Following the cessation of hostilities, Dassault refurbished the fifteen surviving aircraft before they were prematurely retired from service in 1993, following the delivery of F/A-18A Hornets from the USA. The aircraft were offered for sale, with Spain being cited as a possible customer. To date, there has been no success with the aircraft remaining in open storage at Ali Al Salem AB.

Qatar Emiri Air Force (Al Quwwait al Jawwiya al Emiri al Qatar)

Qatar, another Gulf state, was the last export customer for the Mirage F1, placing an order for twelve single-seat F1EDA and two twin-seat F1DDA trainers in 1979. Equipped with BF radar warning receivers and VOR aerials, the aircraft were delivered to Qatar in July 1984, wearing an unusual camouflage scheme of dark and light sand with medium blue undersurfaces. The fourteen aircraft, later supplemented with an additional F1DDA trainer as an attrition replacement, equipped 7 Squadron at Doha airport, forming part of 1 Fighter

Top: Mirage F1EDA of the Qatar Emiri Air Force from No.7 Squadron sits in the sun at Doha Air Base in 1986 armed with Matra Magic R550 missiles on the wingtips. (Photo: via Adrian Balch)

Middle: Rare picture of the two-seat Dassault Mirage F1DDA trainer. Aircraft serial QA62-U was one of only three Mirage F1 training aircraft operated. This picture shows to good effect the Sand, Brown and Blue camouflage scheme. (Photo: via Adrian Balch)

Bottom: Dasault Mirage F1EDA, serial QA71-A was the first aircraft to be delivered to the Qatar Emiri Air Force and is seen here in France awaiting delivery in February 1984. (Photo: via Adrian Balch)

Wing. Their mission equipment included MATRA Magic 1 AAMs and COR2 reconnaissance pods for their primary air-policing role. During the first Gulf War, Mirage F1s of the Qatar Emiri air force were declared to the Coalition and began flying operational missions from their base which were apparently limited to local air-defence and did not involve combat over Kuwait or Iraq. In the mid-1990s, the thirteen surviving aircraft were returned to Dassault in part exchange for Mirage 2000-5 fighters and were subsequently purchased by Spain as attrition replacements for the *Ejercito del Aire*.

1 Mirage F1 Operators – Kuwait

Dassault Mirage F1CK, No.710, of the 'Free Kuwait' Air Force, based at Dhahran during the Gulf War in January 1991. The aircraft displays the original desert scheme, and like Kuwait Air Force A-4 Skyhawks at the time, 'FREE KUWAIT' titles. Note that these differed from aircraft to aircraft, as they were hand-applied.

Reference: *Check List No.1, AMD-BA Mirage F1*, DTU: page 111.

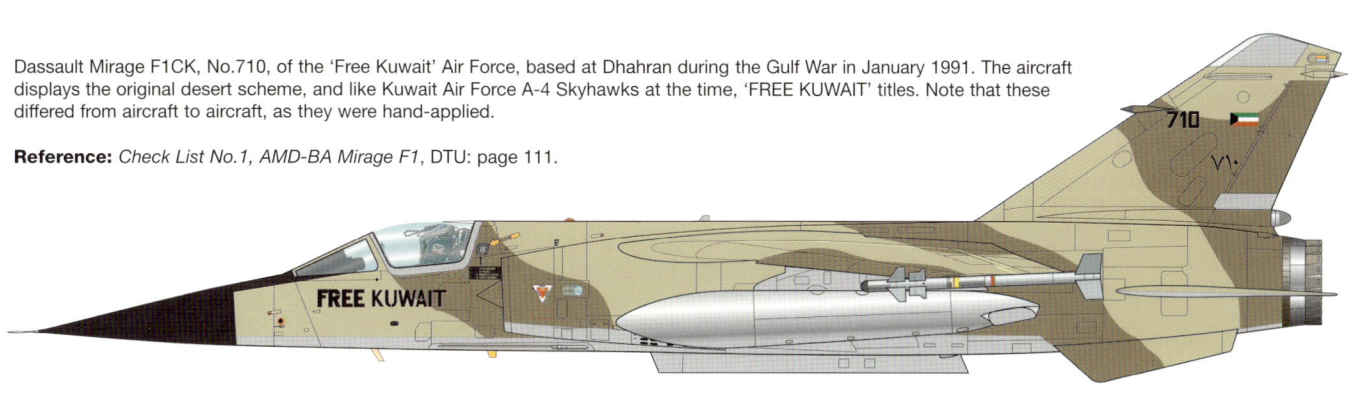

Dassault Mirage F1CK-2, No.722, operated by the Kuwait Air Force *(Al Quwwat al Jawiya al Kuwaitiya)*, during the mid-1990s. This is one of the second production batch (No.719–727) delivered. The aircraft is finished in the later air superiority grey scheme. Two Mk.82SE 500 lb retarded bombs are carried on the centreline.

Reference: *Arab Air Forces*, Squadron Signal Publications: page 31.

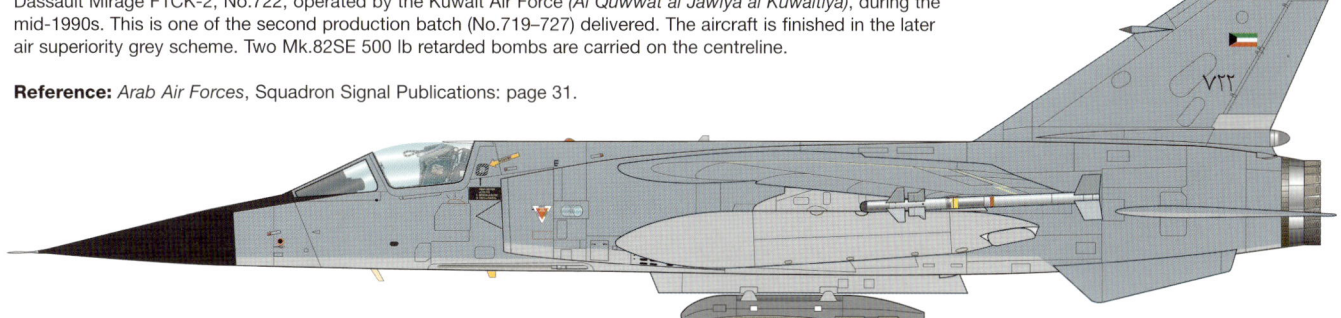

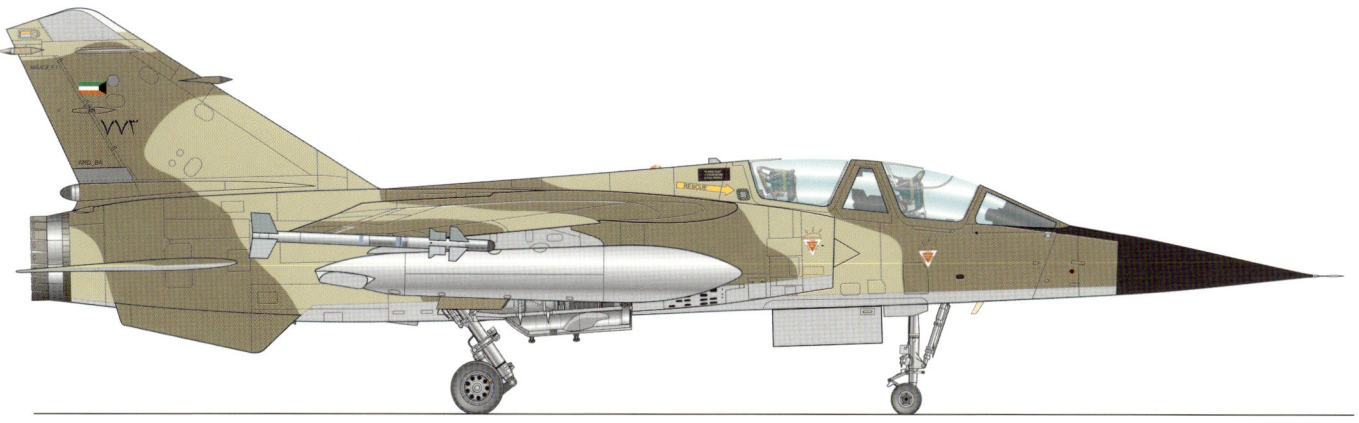

Above and below: Dassault Mirage F1BK, No.773, operated by the Kuwait Air Force *(Al Quwwat al Jawiya al Kuwaitiya)*. The views show the same aircraft in two guises.

Above: the original desert scheme

Below: in the later air superiority grey scheme.

References: *Check List No.1, AMD-BA Mirage F1*, DTU: page 111 (middle photograph. *Aerofax Minigraph No.17, Dassault Mirage F1*: page 24.

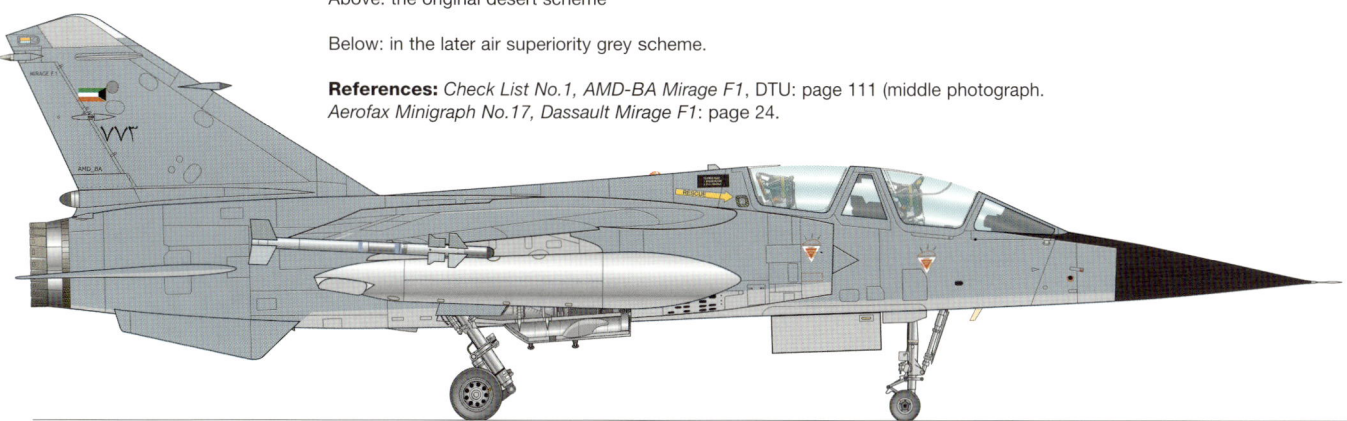

21

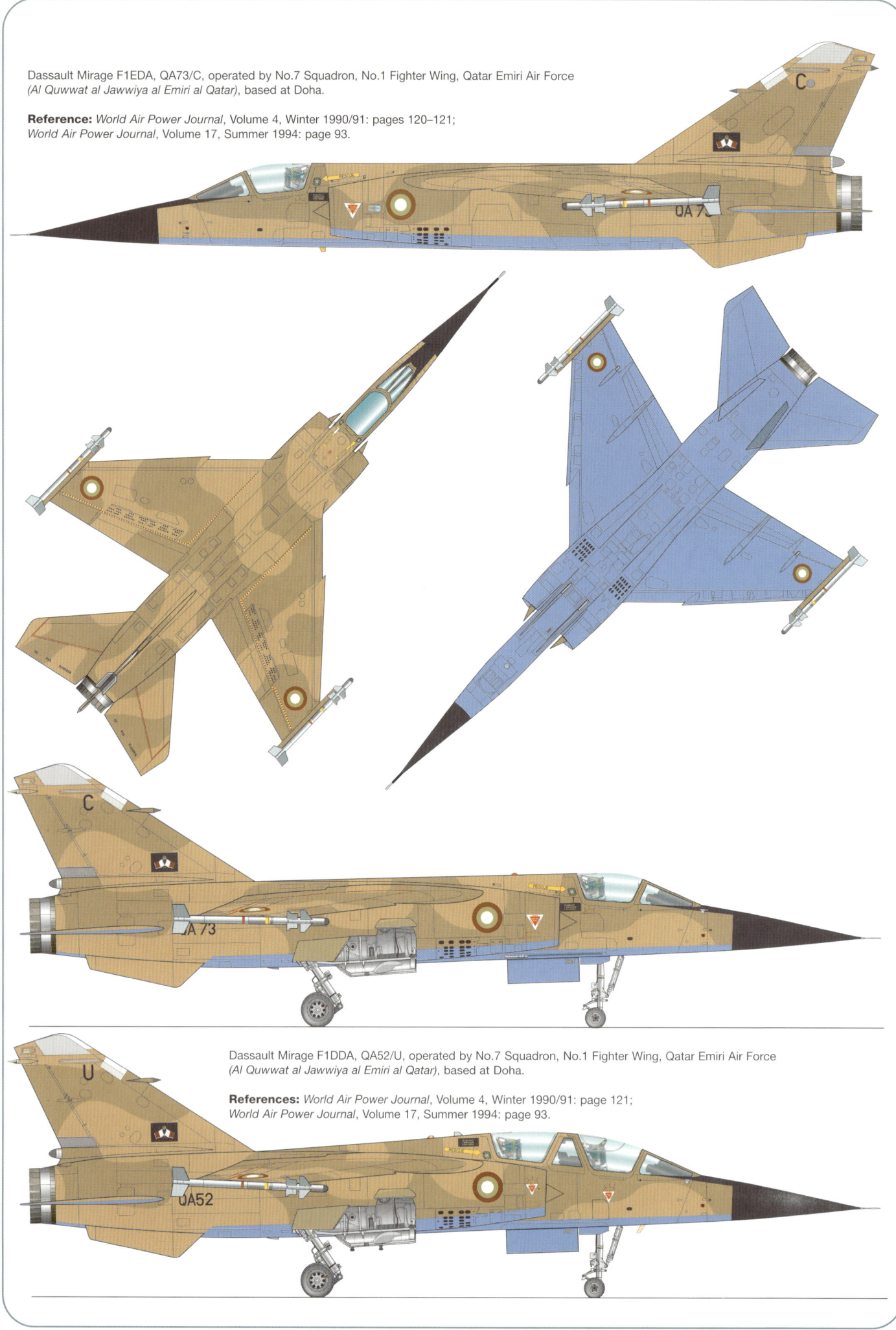

1 Mirage F1 Photopage

A general view of the unique SAAF Mirage F1AZ technology demonstrator (c/n 235) nicknamed 'The World's Fastest Dairy Truck', a reference to the Atlas/Denel corporate colours that the aircraft was finished in which resembled those of a well-known dairy company in South Africa. A detailed walkaround of this particular aircraft appears in Chapter 5. (Photo: Paul Dubois)

A nice head-on shot of a Royal Jordanian Air Force Dassault Mirage F1CJ, based with 25 Squadron at Shaheed Mwaffaq-as-Salti Air Base, Azraq. This photograph clearly shows the sleek aerodynamic lines of this aircraft that sharply contrast with the angular nature of the main undercarriage, a distinctive feature of the Mirage F1. (Photo: Rogier Westerhuis)

A lovely air-to-air shot showing a pair of French Dassault Mirage F1CRs sporting the so-called 'centrafrique' two-tone brown colour scheme used for operations in Chad. Note the Matra 530F missiles mounted on the inboard wing stores pylons. (Photo: via The Aviation Workshop 'Gulf War' Photo Collection)

Armée de l'Air Dassault Mirage F1CR of *ER3/33* (c/n 33-TD/646) high above the snow-capped mountains over Southern Turkey during Operation *Northern Watch*, the UN enforcement of 'No-Fly Zones' over northern Iraq. (Photo: B Colin)

Armée de l'Air Dassault Mirage F1CRs are regular participants at the US-sponsored Exercise *Red Flag* at Nellis AFB, Nevada. This particular Mirage F1CR (c/n 33-NF/605) of *ER2/33* 'Savoie', wearing a two-tone brown and sand colour scheme optimised for desert operations carries two drop tanks and a Phimat pod on the wing pylons with a practice bomb carrier mounted on the centreline. (Photo: The Aviation Workshop 'Gulf War' Collection)

Ecuador Air Force (Fuerza Aerea Ecuatoriana)

Ecuador became the first and only South American nation to order the Mirage F1 when it placed an order for sixteen single-seat F1JAs, based on the F1E, and two F1JE trainers in late 1977, following an unsuccessful attempt to procure the IAI Kfir which had been blocked by the American government. The Mirage F1s were delivered between December 1978 and December 1979 to Base Aerea Taura, Guayaquil where they re-equipped *Escuadron de Caza 2112*, a component of *Grupo 211*, *Ala de Combate 21*, which had previously operated the Cessna A-37B Dragonfly. Just over a year later, in 1981, the Mirage F1JAs were actively involved in flying combat air patrols during the thirteen-day border skirmish between Ecuador and Peru, and on at least one occasion a MATRA Magic 1 air-to-air missile was launched against Peruvian Su-22 'Fitter Fs', apparently without success. Subsequently, on 10 February 1995, the same types clashed again and on this occasion the F1JAs reportedly downed two of the Peruvian jets, although other sources claim one of the aircraft lost was actually an A-37B Dragonfly. The surviving examples of the *Fuerza Aerea Ecuatoriana* Mirage F1 fleet underwent a upgrade programme, with Israeli assistance, during the late 1980s and early 1990s which included modifications to enable the carriage of Israeli-made munitions including Python Mk.III air-to-air missiles which were mounted on the outer underwing pylons and up to eight P-1 bombs on fuselage and wing pylons. The Ecuadorian Mirage F1Jas continue to operate with *Escuadron de Caza 2112*.

Close up of the special markings applied to FAE806. Note also the RWR fairing fitted to the nose of this aircraft which bears a close resemblance to that fitted to SAAF examples. (Photo: Aviation Workshop Archives)

Dassault Mirage F.1JA (c/n FAE806) of *Escuadron de Caza 2112, Grupo 211*. This particular aircraft wears special nose titles and a Su-22 kill marking, the result of a clash with the Peruvian Air Force Su-22 'Fitters' in 1981. (Photo: Aviation Workshop Archives)

Nice air-to-air study of an Ecuadorian Mirage F1JA. The camouflage scheme applied to the Ecuadorian Mirage F1s is rather unique amongst operators of this aircraft. (Photo: Jim Smithe, 'AirPress Photos')

1 Mirage F1 Operators – Ecuador

Dassault Mirage F1JA, FAE809, operated by *Escuadron 2122, Gruppo 211*, Ecuador Air Force *(Fuerza Aerea Ecuatoriana)*, based at Aerea Taura. It is not clear if the aircraft carries the unit badge on the starboard side.

Reference: *World Air Power Journal*, Volume 17, Summer 1994: front cover and page 88.

Dassault Mirage F1JE, FAE830, operated by *Escuadron 2122, Gruppo 211*, Ecuador Air Force *(Fuerza Aerea Ecuatoriana)*, possibly based at Aerea Taura. Aircraft is shown as it appeared just after delivery in March 1979.

Reference: *Aerofax Minigraph No.17, Dassault Mirage F1*: page 15.

25

Spanish Air Force (Ejercito Del Aire)

After protracted negotiations, Spain became the second export customer in Europe to order the Mirage F1, placing an initial order for fifteen F1CE interceptors, given the local designation C.14A, which were delivered between March 1975 and May 1976. Another thirty F1CEs were subsequently ordered together with six two-seat F1BE trainers, designated CE.14As in Spanish service. A further twenty-two orders for the multi-role F1EE variant, for delivery between June 1978 and March 1983, made Spain one of the largest export customers for the aircraft.

The C.14A and CE.14A aircraft eventually equipped *Escuadron 141* 'Chico' and *Escuadron 142* 'Dardo' of *Ala de Caza 14* at Albacete/Los Lllanos and were assigned to the air-defence of mainland Spain. They were initially delivered in a three-tone upper surface camouflage scheme of Dark Brown, Sand and Dark Green over Pale Grey undersurfaces. The C.14B multi-role aircraft were operated by *Escuadron 462* 'Halcones' of *Ala de Caza 11* from Gandos/Las Palmas on the Canary Islands as part of Eastern Air Command and were distinguished by their Blue Grey (FS 35164) and Matt Aluminium colour scheme. All three variants were fitted with BF Radar Warning Receivers and VOR/ILS aerials and the C.14Bs also sported fixed in-flight refuelling probes. Air-defence weapons included either AIM-9P or MATRA 550 Magic short-range AAMs or the medium-range MATRA R.530. For their ground-attack role, Spanish Mirages could be equipped with an external CC-420 30 mm cannon pod to supplement the internal guns. Other weapon options included the CEM-1 multi-store dispenser, BAP100 bomblets or Durandal anti-airfield munitions. The C.14Bs could also be equipped with the Thomson-CSF TMV-018 Syrel ESM/ELINT pod, which has now been accepted fleet-wide on the F1M.

In January 1992, all of the aircraft were unified into *Ala 14* although *Escuadron 462* continued to use the aircraft in *Ala 14* markings up to March 1999 when the unit was re-equipped with the EF18A (C.15) Hornet. The aggregation of Mirage F1 assets was also partly due to an alarming early attrition rate – fifteen aircraft had been lost in accidents by 1993. The Spanish Mirage F1 fleet also started to receive a new Air Superiority Grey overall colour scheme with toned down national and unit markings and this was steadily applied to the majority of the original fleet of C.14As and C.14Bs during major overhauls.

A planned upgrade of the remaining *Ejercito del Aire* Mirage III aircraft was cancelled and by the early 1990s the *Ejercito del Aire* committed itself to the long-term operation of the Mirage F1. Thirteen ex-Qatari Mirage F1s were purchased to re-equip *Ala 11*, a former Mirage III unit, based at Manises. Pending delivery on 1 October 1992 of the Qatari aircraft, ten single-seat F1EDA (one crashed prior to delivery) and two twin-seat F1DDA examples, *Ala 11* operated Mirage C.14s in *Ala 14* markings. With the introduction to service of the 'new' aircraft, the *Ejercito del Aire* added new letter suffixes to their designations. The original F1CE and F1BE became C.14A and CE.14As and the F1EE was designated C.14B. The ex-Qatari machines (F1EDA and F1DDA) became C.14C and CE.14C respectively. The C.14C and CE.14C retained their original Qatari colour schemes, but subsequently received *Ala 11* markings and were operated until 1998 when their base at Manises-Valencia was closed, the unit disbanded and the aircraft were incorporated into *Ala 14* Wing at Los Llanos. In the meantime, the *Ejercito del Aire* had acquired a further four F1Cs and a single two-seat F1B from the *Armée de l'Air* as attrition replacements. The restructuring of the Spanish Mirage F1 fleet eventually led to *Ala 14* operating no less than seven sub-types of the aircraft, making it extremely difficult for pilots to retain currency or for technicians to maintain aircraft with small but significant differences in equipment fits, etc.

In the late 1990s, the *Ejercito del Aire* embarked on an ambitious modernisation programme, based on the avionics upgrade originally intended for SAAF Mirage F1AZs, which involved fifty-five aircraft. At the same time, the majority of ex-Qatari aircraft were retired from service to act as a spares source since their original avionics fit was quite different from that of the other Spanish aircraft and conversion was deemed to be uneconomical. A service life extension and upgrade programme was drawn up with Thomson-CSF selected as the main contractor for the modernisation programme to produce the Mirage F1M (Modernizado). The main part of the upgrade involved the installation of digital avionics, which has greatly improved the mission capability of the Mirage F1, providing the *Ejercito del Aire* with a very effective stop-gap capability pending the arrival of the Eurofighter Typhoon. A new navigation/attack

This Mirage F1CE, coded C.14.18/14-18, belongs to *Ala de Caza 14* of the *Ejercito del Aire* and is seen in the original tactical colour scheme worn by the Spanish variant. The three-tone upper surface camouflage scheme comprised Sand (FS 20400), Dark Brown (FS 20219) and Green (FS 34079) with Pale Grey (FS 36622) undersides. Note the zaps on the forward fuselage.

This Mirage F1M, serialled C.14.54/14-54, actually entered service with the *Ejercito del Aire* as one of twenty-two multi-role F1EE-200s, known by their local designation as C.14Bs. The aircraft were delivered to the *Ejercito del Aire* between October 1981 and March 1983 allowing Spain to form three squadrons within *Ala de Caza 14* and *46*. This particular aircraft belongs to *Escuadron de Caza 142*, a member of the NATO Tiger Association, which explains the presence of a tiger-striped drop tank on the centreline stores pylon. Although this photograph was taken in the late 1990s, by which time most of the *Ejercito del Aire's* Mirage F1s had adopted the low-visibility grey colour scheme, this particular aircraft retained Blue Grey (FS 35164) upper surfaces with Matt Aluminium undersides. National markings included roundels in six positions with a black cross on white top section of the rudder.

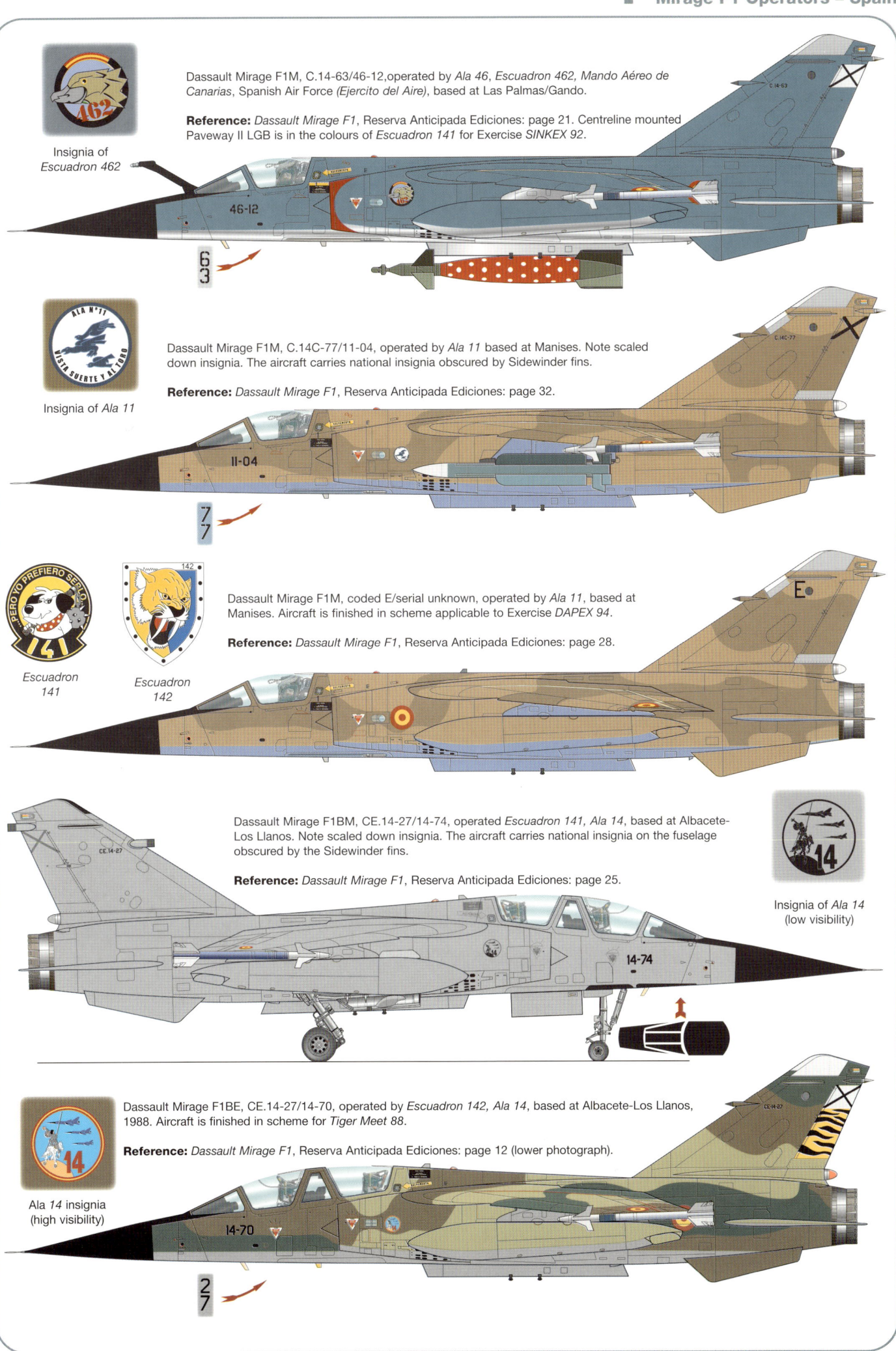

Mirage F1 Operators – Spain

A recently upgraded Mirage F1M, coded C.14.72/14-44 of *Ala de Caza 14*. The aircraft retains the Air Superiority Grey colour scheme with the leading edges of the mainplane, tailerons and fin finished in Corogard Grey. However, it has yet to acquire the new toned-down grey markings or nose radome. Note the revised fairings on the fin leading/trailing edge surfaces and the new Defensive Aids Suite (DAS) fairing alongside the ventral strake that distinguish the upgraded aircraft.

Three views of *Ejercito del Aire* Mirage F1Ms during the annual NATO Tiger Meet in 2004. By the time these particular photographs were taken, the air-defence grey camouflage scheme had been extended to include the nose radome. Note the tiger-striped centreline drop tanks carried by all of these aircraft.

1 Mirage F1 Operators – Spain

system, with an improved Inertial Navigation System (INS), GPS, Smart HUD and Hands on Throttle and Stick (HOTAS) has provided the Mirage F1 Wing with a quantum leap in its ability to conduct the ground-attack mission. Two external changes distinguish the Mirage F1M from its predecessors. Two small black antennae for the AN/ALR-300 Radar Warning Receiver (RWR) are evident on the leading and trailing edges of the fin and under the fuselage ventral fins there are a pair of AN/ALE-40 chaff/flare dispensers. The secondary air-defence role of *Ala 14* Wing has also been enhanced now that all the aircraft possess an active ECM system, previously only available on the C.14B fleet. At least twenty-eight C.14As, seventeen C.14Bs and the four ex-*Armée de l'Air* F1Cs have now been converted to F1M standard. Four two-seat aircraft have similarly been upgraded to F1BM standard, although they have not received the full avionics suite and are not, therefore, combat capable. All of the aircraft now sport the overall air-superiority grey colour scheme, which on some aircraft has been extended to include the nose radome. In spite of the fact that the *Ejercito del Aire* is now starting to take delivery of Eurofighter Typhoon, the highly capable Mirage F1M is now expected to remain in service until at least 2015.

This yet-to-be-modified Mirage F1CE/C.14A, serialled C-14.43/14-43 was one of a second batch of standard interceptor variants delivered to the *Ejercito del Aire* between March 1980 and December 1981. The aircraft wears an overall Air Superiority Grey (FS 36622) colour scheme with black codes, serials and unit badges. Note the fake cockpit markings under the forward fuselage.

A two-seat F1CE/C.14B (C.14.27/14-74) being prepared for another training flight at Albacete. This particular aircraft bears witness to the fact that, contrary to popular belief, the aircraft serial numbers and individual codes do not now always follow suit. Of particular interest in this photograph is the CC-420 30 mm cannon pod, which has been fitted to the centreline stores pylon in preparation for some range work.

This ex-Qatari Mirage F1EDA is one of thirteen survivors that was transferred to the Spanish *Ejercito del Aire*, where they are known as the 'Qataries'. In *Ejercito del Aire* service, the aircraft are now designated C.14Cs to distinguish them from 'standard' aircraft. This aircraft, clearly photographed on the flightline at Albacete soon after arrival in Spain, retains its original 'desert' camouflage scheme of Sand (FS 35250) and Dark Brown (FS 20117) upper surfaces with rather unusual middle blue (FS 35231) undersurfaces, which were peculiar to the Qatari aircraft. The original Qatari tail code (F) that sits high on the fin in black has been retained and the only apparent modification to the markings is the application of large national markings in six positions on the fuselage and wings.

Mirage F1 Operators – Greece

Hellenic Air Force *(Elliniki Polemiki Aeroporia)*

The Dassault Mirage F1s entry into service with the Greek *Elliniki Polemiki Aeroporia* in February 1975 was prompted by growing tensions with Turkey and American political intransigence. Greece had ordered forty Mirage F1CG in June 1974 and the French Government, eager to generate more sales, diverted the delivery of the first sixteen aircraft from the *Armée de l'Air* in order to fulfil the order. Greece thus became the first export customer for the type and was also one of three export customers (along with South Africa and Morocco) that elected not to order or operate the two-seat trainer variant of the F1. The Hellenic Air Force aircraft, initially modified to take AIM-9J Sidewinders in lieu of the standard MATRA Magic air-to-air missile, were assigned to *114a Pterix Mahis* (Combat Wing) at Tanagra, north-west of Athens, to equip 334 'Thalos' and 342 'Sparta' *Mira* (squadrons). In 1984, Greek aeronautical institutes sought to improve the weapon systems for the aircraft and rewired the outboard underwing pylons to take air-to-air missiles. Further Dassault assistance in 1985 allowed Greek Mirage F1CGs to be subsequently armed with four of the improved AIM-9P-2 AAMs. Aircraft were initially delivered without a BF radar warning receiver but these were subsequently fitted as standard during overhauls with Hellenic Aerospace Industries at Tanagra. In Greek service, the Mirage F1CG wore the standard *Armée de l'Air* 'Mirage Bleu' or 'Aegean Blue' colour scheme which consisted of FS35164 applied to upper surfaces with aluminium or silver-grey undersurfaces. The colour scheme proved to be so effective over the Aegean that in the early 1980s all EPA aircraft assigned to interception duties were painted in the same colour scheme. The availability of new aircraft in the late 1980s, including Mirage 2000s, assigned to the defence of Athens, allowed 334 Mira to redeploy to Heraklion AB on the island of Crete in 1989, where it formed part of *126a Smirna Nakis* (Autonomous Group). The unit's aircraft were regularly scrambled against and encountered Turkish military aircraft violating Greek airspace. One Mirage F1CG was lost in June 1992 when it crashed in the Aegean during an interception and subsequent engagement with Turkish F-16 Fighting Falcons. *334 Mira* disbanded in 2000 and passed its surviving aircraft to *342 Mira*. After almost twenty-eight years of service, the remaining twenty-four Mirage F1CGs were retired from Greek service when *342 Mira* disbanded at Tanagra AB on 30 June 2003.

Dassault Mirage F1CG (c/n 129) of *334 Mira, 114 Pterix* in special anniversary markings. The aircraft wore an overall silver colour scheme with red fuselage stripe and a caricature of the Greek god Thalos on the fin, together with the Hellenic Air Force roundel (Photo: Stuart Haigh)

Another specially marked Mirage F1CG (c/n 115), wearing a rather smart yellow and blue colour scheme with a large rendition of the Greek flag running down the fuselage sides and which carried the name "Sparta". This was the last Dassault Mirage F1CG to fly with the Hellenic Air Force when it was retired in June 2003. (Photo: Stuart Haigh)

Hellenic Air Force F1CG (c/n 114) in the standard camouflage scheme worn by the type in Greek service. Note that the code number is repeated on the fuselage sides. (Photo: via Adrian Balch)

1 Mirage F1 Operators – Greece

Dassault Mirage F1CG, No.111, 'Rodos' (Rhodes), operated by *342 Mira, 114 Pterix*, based at Tanagra. Aircraft of this unit carry the names of Greek Islands on the nose just below the windscreen. Other examples include No.103 'Skyros' and No.140 'Crete'.

Reference: *World Air Power Journal*, Volume 17, Summer 1994: page 89.

'Rodos' (Rhodes)

'Polemiki Aeroporia' (War Aviation) titles

At least two Mirage F1CGs recieved the 'Fantasma' (Ghost) scheme as applied to Greek F-16s and some Phantoms. This one operated with *342 Mira*.

Dassault Mirage F1CG, No.129, operated by *334 Mira, 114 Pterix*, (in special anniversary markings), Hellenic Air Force *(Elleniki Polemiki Aeroporia)*. Aircraft was named 'Thalos'.

starboard   port

'Thalos' figure

Dassault Mirage F1CG, No.115, operated by *342 Mira, 114 Pterix*, seen at Hellenic Air Force Open Day 2003 at Tanagra Air Base in June 2003. The aircraft was named 'Sparta' and was the last Mirage F1CG to fly in June 2003.

Starboard

'Sparta' tail marking (port)

1 Mirage F1 Operators – Squadron and Unit Badges

Squadron and Unit Badges

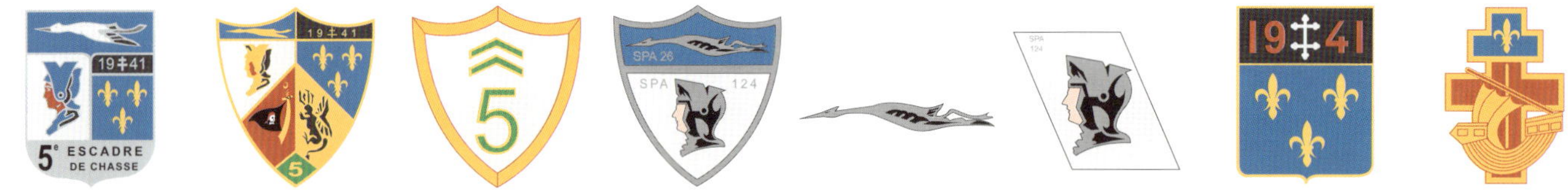

5ème Escadre de Chasse: to 1981

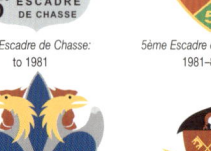

5ème Escadre de Chasse: 1981–85

5ème Escadre de Chasse: 1987 on

Escadre de Chasse 1/5: July 74–Jan 88

1ère Escadrille SPA26 'Cicogne de St. Galmier'

2ème Escadrille SPA124 'Jeanne d'Arc'

Escadron de Chasse 2/5 'Ile de France': July 75–Apr 89

1ère Escadrille 'Paris': not shown

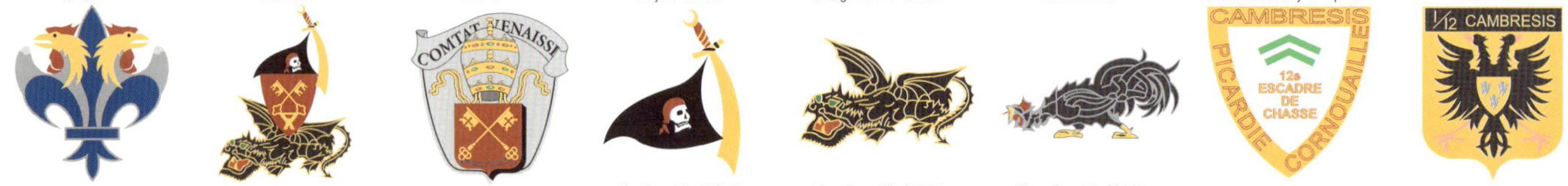

2ème Escadrille 'Versailles' not shown

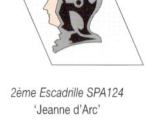

Escadron 3/5: 1985

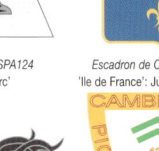

Escadron 3/5: 1988

1ère Escadrille ERC571 'Fanion Pirate'

2ème Escadrille SPA171 'Dragon'

3ème Escadrille SPA62 'Coq de Combat' (Fighting Cock)

12ème Escadre de Chasse 'Picardie Cornouaille'

Escadron de Chasse 1/12 'Cambresis'

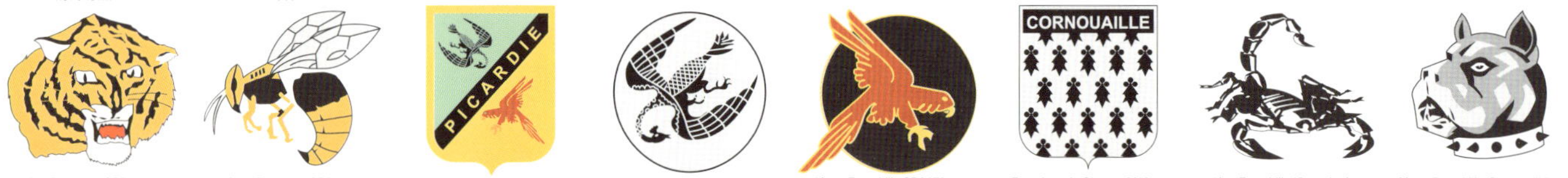

1ère Escadrille SPA162 'Tigre' (Tiger)

2ème Escadrille SPA89 'Guèpe' (Wasp)

Escadron de Chasse 2/12 'Picardie'

1ère Escadrille SPA173 'Oiseau de Paradis' (Bird of Paradise)

2ème Escadrille SPA172 'Perroquet' (Parrot)

Escadron de Chasse 2/12 'Cornouaille'

1ère Escadrille 'Scorpion'

2ème Escadrille 'Dogue d'Ulm' (Bull Mastiff)

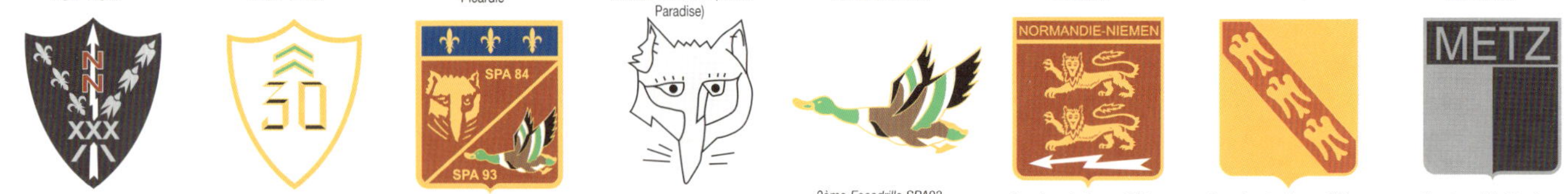

30ème Escadre de Chasse: to 1988

30ème Escadre de Chasse: from 1988

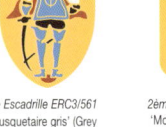

Escadron de Chasse 1/10 'Valois'

1ère Escadrille SPA84 'Renard' (Fox)

2ème Escadrille SPA93 'Col-Vert' (Wild Duck)

Escadron de Chasse 2/30 'Normandie Niémen'

Escadron de Chasse 3/30 'Lorraine'

1ère Escadrille 'Metz': not shown

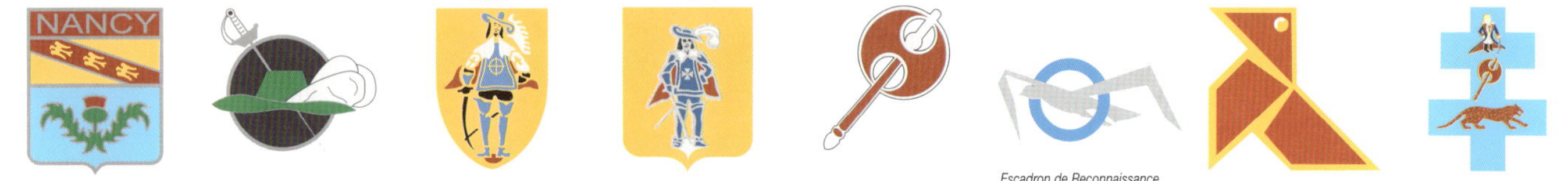

2ème Escadrille 'Nancy': not shown

Escadron de Chasse 4/30 'Vexin'

1ère Escadrille ERC3/561 'Mousquetaire gris' (Grey Musketeer)

2ème Escadrille ERC4/561 'Mousquetaire bleu' (Blue Musketeer)

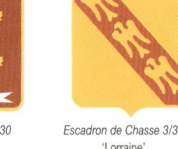

Escadron de Reconnaissance 1/33 'Belfort' (SAL33 'Hache d'abordage' (Boarding Axe))

Escadron de Reconnaissance 2/33 'Mouette du Rhin (Rhine Gull)

BR11 'Cocotte' (Paper Bird)

Escadron de Reconnaissance 1/33 'Belfort'

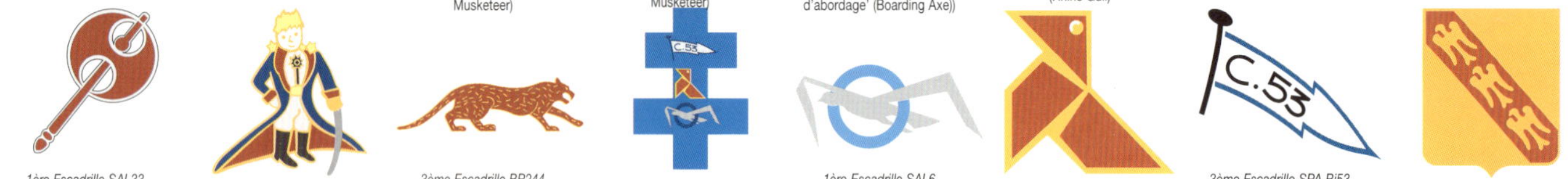

1ère Escadrille SAL33 Hache d'Abordage (Boarding Axe)

2ème Escadrille EALA 9/72 'Petit Prince'

3ème Escadrille BR244 'Leopard'

Escadron de Reconnaissance 2/33 'Savoie'

1ère Escadrille SAL6 'Mouette du Rhin' (Rhine Gull)

2ème Escadrille BR11 'Cocotte' (Paper Bird)

3ème Escadrille SPA Bi53 C53 'Fanion'

Escadron de Chasse 3/33 'Lorraine'

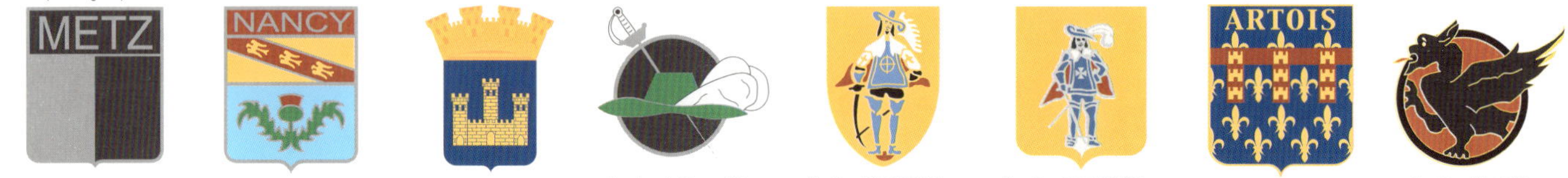

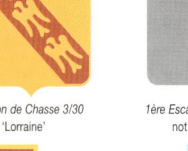

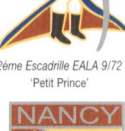

1ère Escadrille 'Metz':

2ème Escadrille 'Nancy':

3ème Escadrille 'Thionville'

Escadron de Chasse 4/33 'Vexin'

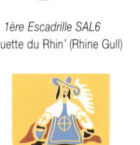

1ère Escadrille ERC3/561 'Mousquetaire gris' (Grey Musketeer)

2ème Escadrille ERC4/561 'Mousquetaire noir'

Escadron de Chasse 1/13 'Artois'

1ère Escadrille SPA83 'Chimère' (Chimera)

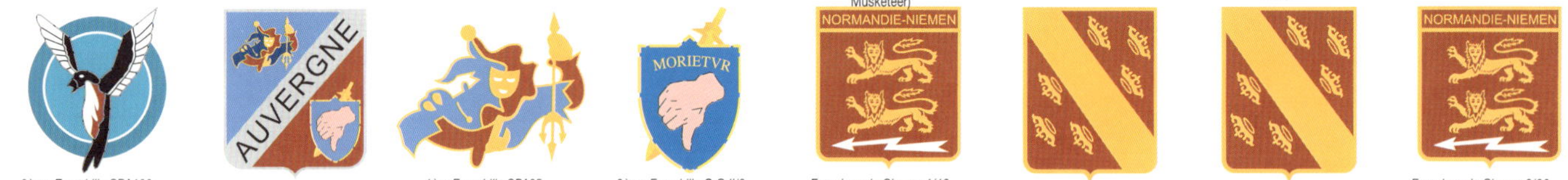

2ème Escadrille SPA100 'Hirondelle' (Sparrow)

Escadron de Chasse 3/13 'Auvergne'

1ère Escadrille SPA85 'La Folie' (Jester)

2ème Escadrille G.C.II/9 'Morietur'

Escadron de Chasse 1/13 'Normandie Niémen': Aug 93 to July 95

Escadron de Chasse 3/13 'Alsace': Aug 93 to July 95

Escadron de Chasse 1/30 'Alsace': from July 95

Escadron de Chasse 2/30 'Normandie Niémen': from July 95

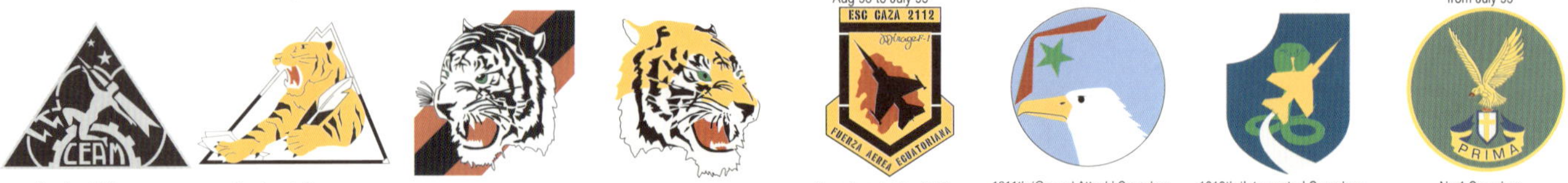

Escadron de Chasse 24/118 (CEAM)

Escadron de Chasse 05/330 'Cote d'Argent'

SPA163 'Siberian Tiger'

SPA164 'Bengal Tiger'

Escuadron de Caza 2112 (Ecuador)

1011th 'Ground Attack' Squadron (Libya)

1012th 'Interceptor' Squadron (Libya)

No.1 Squadron (South Africa)

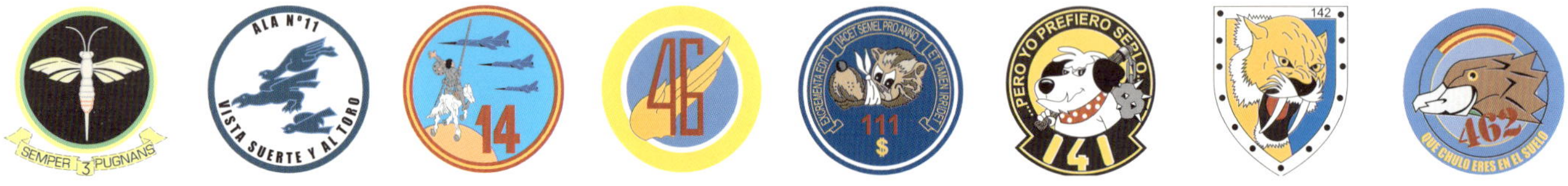

No.3 Squadron (South Africa)

Ala 11 (Spain)

Ala 14 (Spain)

Ala 46 (Spain)

111 Escuadron (Spain)

141 Escuadron (Spain)

142 Escuadron (Spain)

462 Escuadron (Spain)

South African Air Force in Angola and the Bush Wars

During the 1960s, South Africa became increasingly concerned about the long war of independence being fought between the Portuguese and the principal liberation groups (The FNLA[1], MPLA and UNITA) in the neighbouring state of Angola. They were particularly concerned about the growing influence of communism in the region and contributed covert support to Portugal in its long armed conflict with the three main protagonists. Ironically, by April 1974, when a military coup overthrew the dictatorship in Portugal, all three liberation groups had been all but defeated and had retreated to the area that bordered South Africa. The new Portuguese government, tired with the conflict in Angola, withdrew its forces, granted Angola independence in 1975 and handed over political power to a coalition of the three movements. This coalition, unable to agree on governing the newly independent state, quickly broke down and entered into a long civil war during 1976. In a war of ideologies, the MPLA continued to enjoy the support of Cuba and the Soviet Union whilst South Africa, with US assistance, backed the FNLA and UNITA, in an effort to contain the conflict and the spread of communism. Almost simultaneously, South Africa had to contend with the growth of the South West African Peoples Organisation (SWAPO), a liberation group seeking independence for Namibia, a former British colony known as South-West Africa (SWA), which had been handed over to South Africa. During the 1960s and early 1970s SWAPO was based in Zambia, using guerrilla tactics against the South African military, before moving to Angola in 1975 where the Organisation allied itself with their fellow Marxists in the MPLA. Mozambique, another former Portuguese colony to the north-east of South Africa, was backed by the Soviet Union and was seen as another threat although the new nation was struggling with its principal rival, Rhodesia. Thus, by the late 1970s, South Africa was faced with serious challenges to her security across a large part of her northern borders and it was clear that adopting purely defensive measures along the vast border area with insufficient military force was ineffective and not sustainable.

South Africa commenced combat operations against SWAPO targets in Angola from August 1976 with the launch of Operation *Savannah*. Although its argument was chiefly with SWAPO over territorial rights in SWA, the South Africans eventually found themselves also confronting FAPLA (Angolan Government Forces), which had declared their support for SWAPO.

The Mirage F1, only recently introduced to service with the SAAF, entered the so-called 'Bush War' almost by default. In May 1978, South African forces launched Operation *Reindeer* following dramatic incursions into SWA by SWAPO forces, backed by the Angolans. On 6 July, a Mirage F1AZ from No.1 Squadron accompanied a No.2 Squadron Mirage IIIR2Z on a reconnaissance mission into Zambia, effectively flying the first operational sortie performed by the F1 in SAAF service. Just over two years of operational work-up for the South African Mirage F1AZ and F1CZ fleets at AFB Waterkloof culminated in the first of many operational deployments to AFB Ondangwa, a Forward Operating Base (FOB) in South-West Africa as the country ended thirteen years of low-intensity, counter-insurgency bush war and prepared the way for a more intensive campaign against the guerrillas.

Early in 1979, government authority was granted to start launching pre-emptive strikes against SWAPO positions inside Zambian territory after a series of attacks against military targets and the civilian population in the border areas. The Mirage F1CZs were initially tasked to fly combat air patrols over Canberra bombers and Mirage III reconnaissance aircraft, directly supporting the ground units involved in cross border operations during Operation *Rekstok* and *Safran*. As the air-land campaign against SWAPO developed and became ever more sophisticated and the SAAF gained more experience on the relatively new aircraft, so the Mirage F1 force found itself employed in a wider range of missions. Close-escort tasks in support of Buccaneer and Canberra bombers were soon supplemented by strike-attack missions deep into Angolan territory, using a mix of Mk.82 bombs and SNEB rockets to strike against established guerrilla camps or targets of opportunity during missions to support the South African Army. Close air support was principally conducted by the slower moving Impala[2], although the ground threat environment was becoming ever more sophisticated. On 7 June 1980, the Mirage F1 demonstrated its survivability when two aircraft (F1AZ c/ns 234 and 237) were hit almost simultaneously, by separate SA-7 SAMs over a target near Lubango, both safely recovering to SAAF FOBs in SWA. The SAAF Mirage F1s continued to be employed on a wide range of tasks during the carefully orchestrated campaign of selective strikes against guerrilla forces during 1980–81, during which time the close air Support mission was developed, principally for the F1AZ force of No.1 Squadron. In November 1981, South African forces launched a major strike deep into Angolan territory with the aim of destroying SWAPO's north-eastern headquarters. During this campaign (code-named Operation *Daisy*) on 6 November, the first Mirage F1 air-to-air kill was achieved when a F1CZ flown by Major Johan Rankin shot down an Angolan MiG-21MF, one of a pair that had been scrambled to intercept the Mirage F1s. Major Rankin used cannon fire to bring the aircraft down after AAMs were launched outside their operational envelope. This much celebrated incident was the first SAAF aerial victory since the Korean War. The next twelve months were punctuated by further skirmishes along and inside the border, with regular use of the Mirage F1. On 5 October 1982, a Canberra PR sortie, escorted by two Mirage F1CZs was intercepted by four MiG-21s from Menogue, one of the main Angolan air bases, and in the ensuing brief air battle Major Rankin claimed his second confirmed kill against a MiG-21MF, using a combination of AAMs and 30 mm DEFA cannon fire. The following year, in May 1983, the SAAF Mirages found themselves flying, albeit briefly, over an additional area of operations. Following the detonation of a large car bomb by the African National Congress (ANC) terrorist group outside the SAAF Headquarters in Pretoria which caused large scale casualties, the SAAF launched reprisal raids against ANC camps around Maputo in neighbouring Mozambique during Operation *Skerwe*. The Impala strike-attack aircraft was the principal asset used for these raids but there were concerns about the risks posed by the SA-3 SAM batteries and associated Low Blow radar guidance system defending the city. The Impalas were, therefore, supported by Mirage F1AZs from No.1 Squadron, which destroyed the vital radar guidance systems and subsequently provided top cover for the raids. In spite of this brief interlude, and for the next six years, the SAAF Mirage F1s continued to make a significant contribution to the so-called 'Border War', constantly developing their tactics to

---

[1] FNLA – National Liberation Front of Angola (tribal based). MPLA – Popular Movement for the Liberation of Angola (Marxist-Leninist). UNITA – National Union for the Total Independence of Angola (Maoist).

[2] Licence-built South African version of the Italian Siai-Marchetti MB-326M advanced trainer/light attack aircraft

2 Mirage F1 at War – SAAF in Angola and the Bush Wars

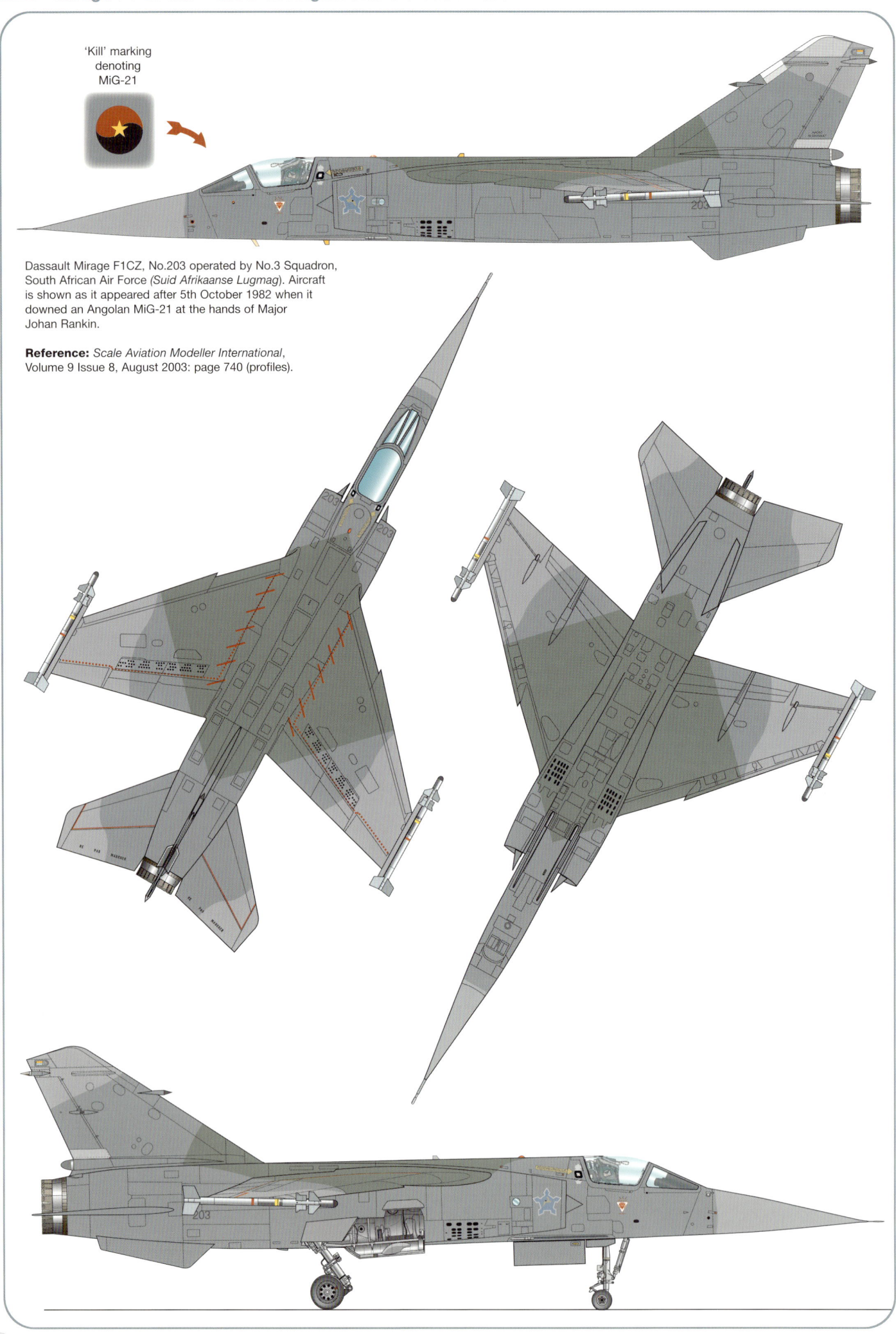

'Kill' marking denoting MiG-21

Dassault Mirage F1CZ, No.203 operated by No.3 Squadron, South African Air Force *(Suid Afrikaanse Lugmag)*. Aircraft is shown as it appeared after 5th October 1982 when it downed an Angolan MiG-21 at the hands of Major Johan Rankin.

Reference: *Scale Aviation Modeller International*, Volume 9 Issue 8, August 2003: page 740 (profiles).

2 Mirage F1 at War – Morrocan Air Force in the Western Sahara

better support the army and combat the increasingly complex air defence system in Angola, recognised as the most sophisticated of Soviet origin outside the Warsaw Pact countries. On 27 September 1987, during Operation *Moduler*, the Angolans clearly demonstrated the near parity that was being reached in the air, when a pair of MiG-23 'Floggers' engaged two Mirage F1CZs. One of the F1CZs (c/n 206) was hit by either an AA-7 or AA-8 missile during the dogfight but the pilot managed to land the aircraft successfully at AFB Rundu. In a strike against two guerrilla strongholds, at Cuito Cuanavale and Lubango on 20 February 1988, the SAAF recorded its first Mirage F1 loss to enemy action when F1AZ (c/n 245) was shot down at low level with a SA-13 SAM and less than a month later another F1AZ (c/n 223) crashed during a low-level night operation in Angola with the loss of the pilot. Ironically, South African involvement in Angola was coming to an end, as talks between the main protagonists in May 1988 resulted in the withdrawal of large numbers of South African and Cuban troops from the country in return for a number of conditions, including eventual independence for Namibia.

Dassault Mirage F1AZ (c/n 209) of No.3 Squadron SAAF, in the original high contrast tactical camouflage colour scheme with high visibility markings. Judging by the condition of this aircraft, it is either a newly delivered example or has recently received a complete overhaul. Note the natural metal centreline drop tanks. (Photo: via Adrain Balch)

Two Mirage F1AZs outside their maintenance hangar. This photo was obviously taken during the transition phase between the application of tactical colour schemes to SAAF aircraft. The aircraft in the foreground wears the old high-contrast camouflage scheme with high visibility markings. The aircraft in the background wears the later, low-visibility scheme and markings. (Photo: Paul Dubois)

Dassault Mirage F1AZ (c/n 228) of No.3 Squadron SAAF. Another very clean looking example, as is the aircraft in the background, which suggests that this photograph was taken shortly after delivery of these aircraft. The harsh operational environment over south-western Africa and Angola would soon take their toll on the appearance of these aircraft. (Photo: via Adrain Balch)

Royal Moroccan Air Force (*Al Kuwwat al Jawwiya al Malakiya Marakishiya*) in the Western Sahara

In 1974, Spain announced that she would withdraw from Spanish Sahara and the neighbouring states, Morocco and Mauretania, subsequently agreed on partition. Spain had previously held talks with the Algerian-backed Popular Front for the Liberation of Saguiet el-Hamra and Rio de Oro (*Polisario*) seeking a political solution. After clashes between Moroccan and Algerian troops and the final withdrawal of Spanish forces from the disputed territories, Mauretania and Morocco occupied south and north Spanish Sahara respectively and *Polisario* forces started attacking regular forces. The fighting intensified and the Royal Moroccan Air Force (*Al Kuwwat al Jawwiya al Malakiya Marakishiya*) lost a number of aircraft in skirmishes with Polisario forces. The urgent need for newer combat aircraft resulted in the early delivery of Mirage F1s, diverted from an order for the French *Armée de l'Air* to the Royal Moroccan Air Force in 1978. These aircraft, which included both air-defence and ground-attack optimised variants were quickly pressed into service against an increasingly sophisticated rebel organisation that was being backed by both Algeria and Libya. The two Moroccan Mirage F1 squadrons operated from their main base at Sidi Slimane, near Meknes in Morocco and a forward operating base at El Aioun in the northern part of the former Spanish Sahara on a wide range of missions, including air-defence, tactical reconnaissance, ground-attack, and close-air-support (CAS). In October 1981, *Polisario* forces launched a major attack against the Moroccan garrison at Guelta Zemmour, on the border between the Western Sahara and Mauretania. The Royal Moroccan Air Force flew dozens of supply and attack sorties in support of their land forces in an effort to repel these attacks. During this time, they lost a C-130H Hercules to a SA-7 attack and, more significantly, two Mirage F1CHs, one of which was flying at high level, which were shot down by SA-8s believed to have been launched from inside Algeria. Polisario forces claimed a third, confirmed, Mirage F1 kill in January 1985 before Morocco relinquished its territorial claims in the Western Sahara. The conflict was brought to an end in August 1988.

Armée de l'Air and Libyan Arab Republic Air Force (Al Quwwat al Jawwiya al Jamahiriya al Arabiya al Libyya) in Chad

Chad gained independence from France in 1960 although French troops remained in the country for many years to support the minority Christian government. The majority of the population, concentrated in the north, is Muslim. Throughout the 1960s and early 1970s, rebel groups contested the Government's authority and, with increasing Libyan support, facilitated a coup in April 1975. The French authorities continued to maintain an interest in Chad, given its strategic importance to them, and military forces were regularly engaged in support of the various regimes that gained power. By 1980, civil war raged in the country and it was seen as a major harbour for terrorists sponsored by Libya. Western concerns over the threat to Sudan and Egypt led the United States and France to continue their, often covert, support to Chad. In the meantime, Mirage F1ADs from the *Al Quwwat al Jawwiya al Jamahiriya al Arabiya al Libyya* were deployed at Marten es-Serra AB, in southern Libya during 1981. Flown by French-trained Libyan, Pakistani and Palestinian pilots, these aircraft were used extensively against opposing forces during the early Libyan campaigns in Chad in 1981 and 1983. Aircraft configured with two 1,300 litre drop tanks and a pair of Belouga CBUs on the centreline pylon were regularly tasked for ground-attack missions. From late 1983, when Operation *Manta* was launched, French *Armée de l'Air* Mirage F1s became more frequent participants in the region and the Libyans, who considered their Mirage F1s as high-value assets, held back their squadrons in the north of the country to avoid 'friendly fire' incidents in the region and to preserve their aircraft for possible confrontations against the growing threat from American carrier groups in the Mediterranean. The *Armée de l'Air* was kept busy with military operations against Libyan-backed rebel groups in the country and Mirage F1Cs were regularly deployed in support of SEPECAT Jaguar ground-attack missions against rebel camps and positions. In Autumn 1984, France and Libya agreed to withdraw from Chad but the latter largely went back on the agreement and continued to support rebel forces. In February 1986, France launched Operation *Epervier* and Mirage F1s, once again, were called upon to act as escorts for Jaguar bombing missions. France subsequently deployed Mirage F1Cs to N'Djamena for a short period before reduced tensions permitted the *Armée de l'Air* to redeploy these assets to neighbouring states. In early 1987, *Armée de l'Air* Mirage F1Cs of EC5 were deployed in support of a strike package against installations at the Libyan-built air base at Ouadi Doum following renewed fighting in the country. Pre- and post-strike reconnaissance was carried out by Mirage F1CRs of ER33, also based at Bangui in the Central African Republic. In September 1987, Chad, backed by France and Zaire, invaded Libya and recaptured disputed territory from Libyan-backed rebels. During attacks on at least one airfield inside Libya, twenty-two combat aircraft were destroyed on the ground although the inclusion of Mirage F1s in the figure cannot be confirmed. Shortly afterwards, the two warring factions agreed a ceasefire although Libyan Air Force aircraft still make occasional over-flights, carefully monitored by French forces still based in the region.

Dassault Mirage F1C-200 (c/n 30-SA) of *EC1/30* 'Valois', home-based at Reims and sporting a two-tone brown camouflage colour scheme for African operations. This particular aircraft, devoid of any unit markings, shows clear evidence of extensive operations in the harsh environment of Central Africa. (Photo: via The Aviation Workshop 'Gulf War' Photo Collection)

2 Mirage F1 at War – Armée de l'Air Libyan Arab Republic Air Force in Chad

Dassault Mirage F1C-200, 30-LD/No.210 operated by *Escadron de Chasse 4/30* 'Vexin'. The aircraft is shown in the scheme it carried during operations over Djibouti, Chad. The lower side view shows the same aircraft as it appeared when the unit was re-classified as *EC4/33* 'Vexin'.

Most of the French Air Force Mirage F1s that were sent wore the camouflage schemes referred to as FaTAC/TCHAD 'Sable Chamois'. There were two versions of this – *Tchad 1ère* and *Tchad 2ème*.

The Libyan aircraft wore the standard camouflage scheme of Tan FS30219, Medium Green FS34102 and Dark Green FS34079 with Grey FS 36622 undersides.

Reference: *Check List No.1, AMD-BA Mirage F1*, DTU: page 23 and page 26

Insignia of *1ère Escadrille*, ERC3/561 'Mousquetaire Gris' (Grey Musketeer).

Insignia of *2ème Escadrille*, ERC4/561 'Mousquetaire Noir' (Black Musketeer)

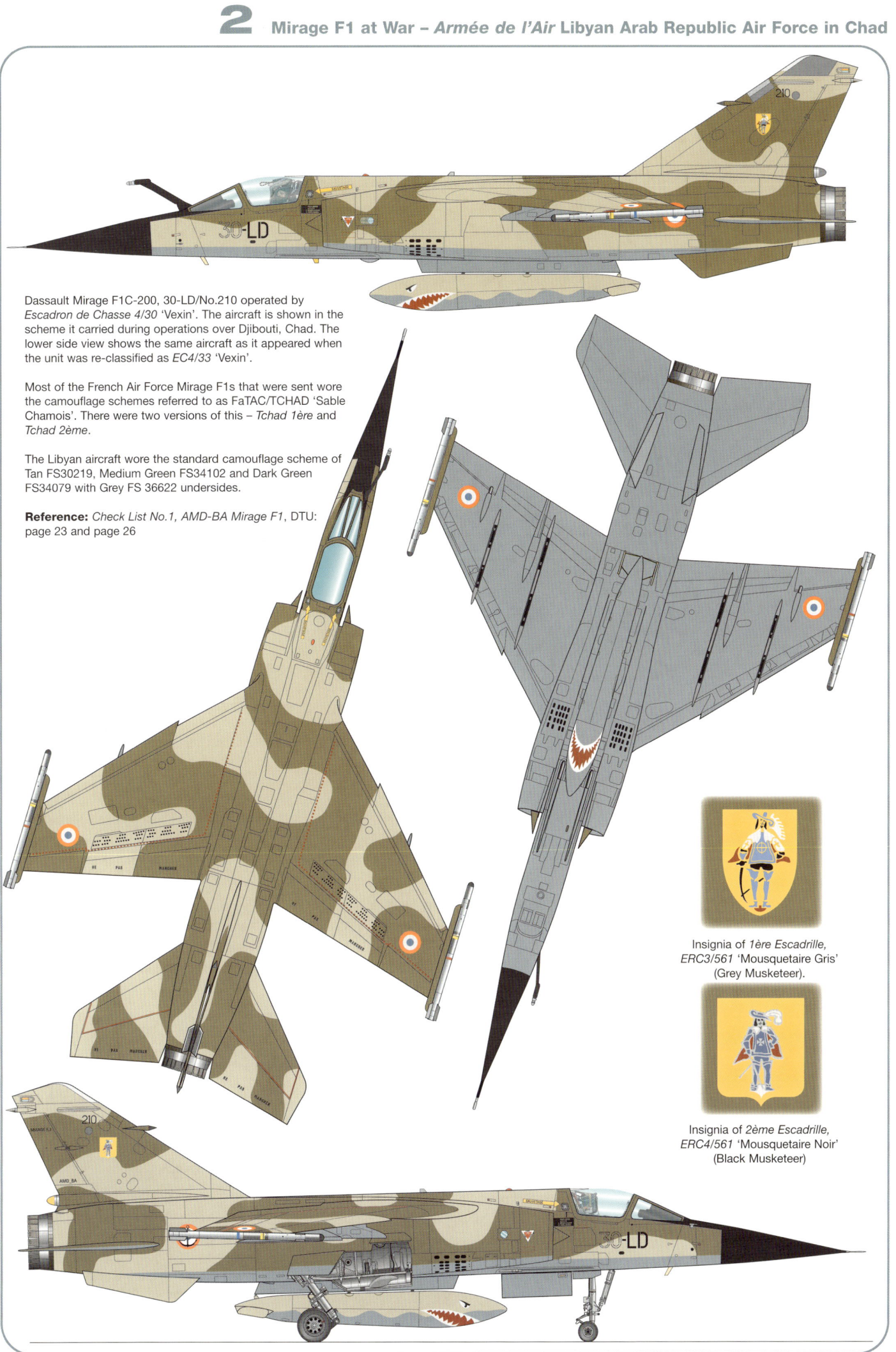

37

Mirage F1 at War – The Iraqi Air Force in the Gulf War with Iran 1980–88

The Iraqi Air Force (*Al Quwwat al Jawwiya al Iraqiya*) in the Gulf War with Iran 1980–88

Initial Iraqi Mirage F1 orders were being fulfilled by France just as the first Gulf War, with Iran, broke out in 1980. France declined to join the international arms embargo and allowed the first aircraft to be delivered to Iraq in January 1981, disguised as a delivery to neighbouring Jordan. The first thirty-two Mirage F1EQs were assigned to air interception duties and their French-trained pilots were considered to be the Iraqi Air Force élite. They exhibited a higher degree of skill than their Soviet-trained counterparts and appeared more willing to engage in air-to-air combat. During the first three years of the war with Iran, the Iraqi F1EQs claimed thirty-five aerial victories using MATRA Super 530s, fired in pairs, or 30 mm DEFA cannons. The majority of their victims appeared to be F-4D/E and RF-4E Phantom IIs or F-5E Tiger II aircraft although at least one Grumman F-14A Tomcat also fell victim to the Mirage F1EQ. Later, more substantiated claims put the final figure for Iraqi Mirage F1EQ kills at eighteen, achieved between April 1982 and July 1988. Iraqi Mirage F1EQs also escorted bombing missions and conducted reconnaissance, flying from Qayyarah West and temporary bases close to the Iran/Iraq front lines in the poorly managed air war against Iran's army.

Iraq's newer Agave/Exocet-equipped Mirage F1EQs, acquired to replace French-loaned Super Etendards, met with more success in the Gulf in the so-called 'Tanker War'. In spite of an initial missile interface problem during the first Mirage F1EQs-4s Exocet-armed mission in December 1984, the Iraqi Air force went on to complete attacks on over one hundred vessels between mid-1984 and the end of he war in August 1988. Once again, French-trained pilots exhibited a high degree of skill and determination when attacking Iranian surface targets. Exocet missiles, many fired from Mirage F1s, were credited with all but four of the forty-one ships destroyed during the 'Tanker War'. This included the highly publicised raid in which an Iraqi F1 fired two Exocet anti-ship missiles at *USS Stark* in May 1987 that resulted in the ship being severely damaged with thirty-seven American sailors losing their lives. It is understood that Mirage F1EQs equipped No.91 Squadron at Kut al-Hayy, 102 Squadron at Qayyarah West and Nos.111 and 112 Squadrons at Qayyarah South during this period. The typical Iraqi Mirage F1EQ-5 configuration for anti-shipping missions over the Persian Gulf consisted of a single AM.39 Exocet missile on the centreline pylon with two RP.15 external underwing fuel tanks. In this configuration, the aircraft were slow and cumbersome to fly and became easy prey for Iranian F-14s so, from 1985, the Iraqis started mounting R.550 missiles, ECM pods and chaff/flare dispensers to improve their survivability but this significantly reduced their effective combat range. In 1986, the Iraqi Air Force introduced two modified Antonov An-12BP tanker aircraft to extend the operational radius of action of the Mirage F1EQs, which aroused suspicions that mercenary pilots were being used for some of the more complex missions since Iraqi Air Force pilots were unfamiliar with the intricate nature of in-flight refuelling operations.

During the final Iraqi offensives of 1988, Mirage F1EQs with PGMs attacked Iranian armaments factories, oil refineries and facilities, bridges and causeways. The extensive use of the Mirage F1EQ force during the major part of the eight-year war with Iran resulted in a high rate of attrition. It is estimated that the Iraqis lost as many as forty Mirage F1EQs between 1981 and 1988 with the worst attrition during the last two years of the war. They lost an estimated ten aircraft in 1987 and no less than fourteen in 1988 including eight in one month. Most of the aircraft were downed by the Grumman F-14A Tomcat, but confirmed F-4E Phantom kills included single aircraft in both February 1986 and March 1988. It is estimated that no more than six of the definitive Mirage F1EQ-6 variant in Iraqi service survived the war with Iran. Last honours did, however, fall to the Iraqi Mirage F1 force which downed an Iranian F-4E Phantom on 19 July 1988, the day that Iran accepted UN Resolution 598 calling for an end to hostilities with Iraq.

Dassault Mirage F1CR of *ER1/33* 'Belfort' taxing out for a reconnaissance mission during Operation *Draguet* from Al Ahsa Air Base in Saudi Arabia. (Photo: via The Aviation Workshop 'Gulf War' Photo Collection)

It is understood that the Islamic Republic of Iran Air Force (IRIAF) may have been operating a number of ex-Iraqi Air Force Dassault Mirage F1EQs that fled to Iran at the height of the Coalition air campaign against Saddam Hussein's regime during Operation *Desert Storm* in early 1991. It has been reported that six examples were tested during 1992–93 and that aircraft were subsequently operated from either Nojeh or Iman Reza AB. The aircraft almost certainly retained their original Iraqi colour schemes with examples in both the three-tone tactical camouflage or maritime Dark/Light Grey colour schemes sighted at Mashad. IRIAF Mirage F1 operations remain obscure although there have been reported sightings of aircraft in a new light grey camouflage pattern similar to that now worn by surviving IRIAF F-14A Tomcats and MiG-29s which would suggest that these aircraft remain operational.

Armée de l'Air and the Iraqi Air Force (*Al Quwwat al Jawwiya al Iraqiya*) in Operation *Desert Storm* 1991

From the beginning of the Gulf crisis in August 1990, when Saddam Hussein ordered Iraqi forces to invade the neighbouring state of Kuwait, the French *Armée de l'Air* was maintained at a high state of readiness, both in France and overseas. This included a fighter squadron in Djibouti, North-East Africa equipped with Mirage F1Cs. On 15 September, France announced their participation in the international coalition that was being assembled to expel Iraqi forces and liberate Kuwait. This operation was code-named Operation *Daguet*. Just over two weeks later, on 3 October, four Dassault Mirage F1CRs of *ECR33* based at Strasbourg, formed part of the lead element deployed to the Middle East. Based at Al Ahsa, a civilian airfield in Saudi Arabia, they were joined by four more aircraft from the same Wing on 8 October.

Simultaneously, France entered into a military agreement with the neighbouring state of Qatar, which included the provision of additional air defence assets to defend this small Arab Emirate. On 17 October, eight Mirage F1Cs of *EC12* from Cambrai-Epinoy deployed to Doha under the code-name Operation *Meteil* where they shared air-defence duties with the Mirage F1EDAs of the Qatari Air Force. Prior to the start of combat operations during Operation *Desert Shield*, a Mirage F1CR from *ER3/33* 'Moselle' was lost with its pilot in a training accident.

After protracted negotiations with Saddam Hussein in late 1990 and early 1991 failed, Coalition forces under the leadership of the United States of America launched Operation *Desert Storm*. The air campaign commenced on 17 January, but the *Armée de l'Air* Mirage F1CRs were initially excluded from combat operations over fears that they could be confused with the F1EQs operated by the Iraqi Air Force. Some ten days later, following large-scale losses of Iraqi Air Force assets in the air and on the ground and a mass exodus of aircraft to neighbouring Iran, the Coalition Air Forces declared air supremacy and it was deemed safe for the *Armée de l'Air* F1CRs to begin combat operations. On 26 January, four F1CRs performed their first bombing mission against Iraqi mechanised units and artillery sites in Kuwait and Iraq. They also completed photographic reconnaissance missions with the new RAPHAEL SLAR (Sideways Looking Airborne Radar) pod. The Mirage F1CR proved to be particular useful in the target designation role flying joint missions with the numerically superior, but less sophisticated, Jaguar fighter-bomber. These combined missions, with the Mirage F1CR using its air-to-ground radar modes, allowed the Jaguars to complete precision attacks on a range of strategic targets in preparation for the allied ground offensive, which began on 24 February. On this day, a mixed force of Mirage F1CRs and Jaguars bombed Tallil Air Base in Iraq and the last combat missions were completed on 27 February. The Mirage F1CRs returned to France in early March 1991 after completing 114 combat sorties, including fifty-one reconnaissance missions. There were no combat losses amongst the *Armée de l'Air* Mirage F1 force, the result of the excellent training and experience acquired during previous operations in Chad and Mauritania (covered elsewhere).

Although some sources estimate that over ninety single-seat Mirage F1s from France remained in service with the Iraqi Air Force in 1991, it is now understood that Iraq had sixty-two Mirage F1EQs and eleven two-seat F1BQs in service at the beginning of Operation *Desert Storm* in January 1991. Some sources also suggest that the Iraqi Air Force acquired between six and eight Kuwaiti Mirage F1s following the August 1990 invasion and that these aircraft were taken to Iraq and used as a source of spares, although this claim can not be corroborated at this time. By 1991, the much vaunted Iraqi Mirage F1 force had lost its edge and a defending Iraqi Mirage F1 was, in fact, the first aircraft to be shot down in the conflict – by a USAF F-15C Eagle on 17 January 1991, the first day of the air campaign. Three others were lost on the same day, two more to F-15Cs and one which crashed avoiding an unarmed GD EF-111A Raven. Another two were destroyed on 19 January with two more on the 24th in a highly publicised engagement with a Royal Saudi Air Force F-15C Eagle. On 26 January, the first of twenty-four Iraqi Mirage F1s took refuge in Iran before the ninth, and last, Mirage F1 to be destroyed in an air-to-air engagement was lost on 27 January, again to a USAF F-15C.

Dassault Mirage F1CR (c/n 646/33-NH) wearing the standard 'Djbouti' sand/brown colour scheme and the 'Mouette du Rhin' (Rhine Gull) unit markings of the *1ére Escadrille* of *ER33*, based at Strasbourg-Entzheim. This clean aircraft has an IFR probe fitted for the long transit flights to/from Djibouti. Note the fairing under the nose that distinguishes the reconnaissance roled F1CR from its fighter-bomber cousins. (Photo: Lindsay Peacock)

2 Mirage F1 at War – *Armée de l'Air* and the Iraqi Air Force in Operation *Desert Storm* 1991

'Oiseau de paradis' (Paradise bird) insignia of *SPA173* (port)

'Perroquet' (Parrot) insignia of *SPA172* (starboard)

Dassault Mirage F1C. 12-KO, No.245, operated by *EC2/12* 'Picardie', based at Doha, Qatar.

Reference: *La Victoire Venue du Ciel*, page 45 (photograph); *World Air Power Journal*, Volume 17, Summer 1994: page 82.

Dassault Mirage F1CR-200, 33-CR, No.622, operated by *ER1/33* 'Belfort', based at based at Strasbourg-Entzheim.

Reference: *La Victoire Venue du Ciel*: page 40.

'Petit Prince' (Little Prince) insignia of 2ème Escadrille, EALA9/72

'Hache d'Abordage' (Boarding Axe) insignia of 1ère Escadrille, SAL33

The French Air Force Mirage F1 fleet carried a mixture of desert camouflage schemes including *Tchad 1ère*, *Tchad 2ème*, Arabia Type A and Arabia Type B. Most aircraft also carried squadron and wing markings in full colour, but reduced in size.

Dassault Mirage F1CR-200, 33-TD, No.646, operated by *ER3/33* 'Moselle' based at Al Ahsa, Saudi Arabia during the Gulf War.

Reference: *World Air Power Journal*, Volume 17, Summer 1994: page 75.

'Cocotte' (Paper Bird) insignia of *ER3/33* 'Moselle'

Insignia of *ER2/33* 'Savoie' carried on both sides of fin until 1993

Dassault Mirage F1CR-200, 33-NL, No.630, operated by *ER2/33* 'Savoie' during Operation *Aconit*.

References: *Check List No.1, AMD-BA Mirage F1*, DTU: page 57 (top photograph); *World Air Power Journal*, Volume 17, Summer 1994: page 86.

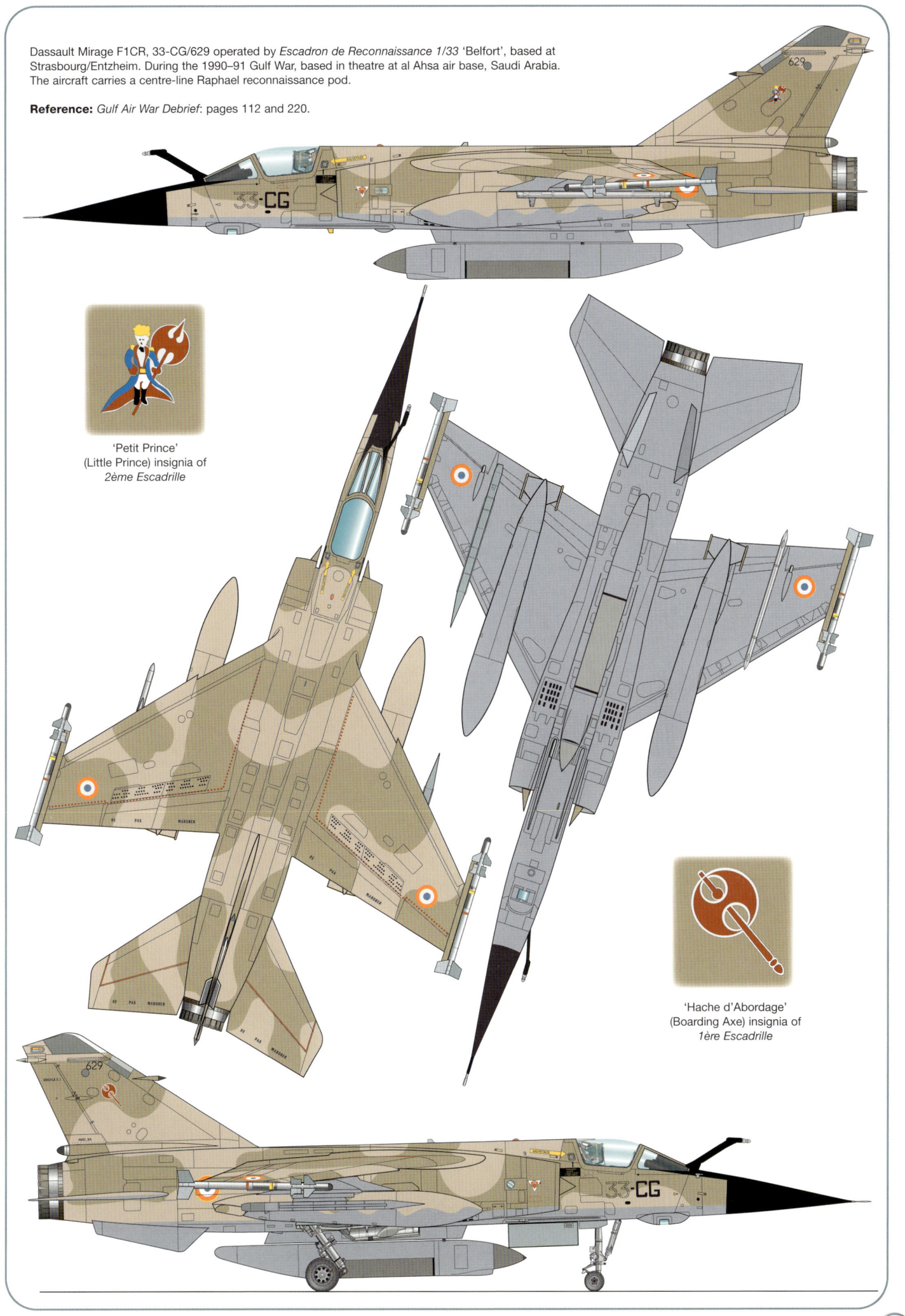

2 Mirage F1 at War – *Armée de l'Air* and the Iraqi Air Force in Operation *Desert Storm* 1991

Dassault Mirage F1CR, 33-CG/629 operated by *Escadron de Reconnaissance 1/33* 'Belfort', based at Strasbourg/Entzheim. During the 1990–91 Gulf War, based in theatre at al Ahsa air base, Saudi Arabia. The aircraft carries a centre-line Raphael reconnaissance pod.

Reference: *Gulf Air War Debrief*: pages 112 and 220.

'Petit Prince'
(Little Prince) insignia of
2ème Escadrille

'Hache d'Abordage'
(Boarding Axe) insignia of
1ère Escadrille

Armée de l'Air in the Balkans Conflict 1995–99

The break up of the former Yugoslavia in the early 1990s was followed by a series of vicious civil wars in the region as ethnic tensions, largely suppressed for the best part of fifty years under Marshall Tito's rule, spilled over. A very brief 'war of independence' in Slovenia was followed by more protracted conflicts, initially in Croatia, then Bosnia-Herzegovina and towards the end of the decade in Kosovo. During October 1992, in an attempt to contain at least some of the fighting taking place in both Croatia and Bosnia-Herzegovina, the United Nations imposed a 'no-fly zone'. This was ignored by the warring factions until NATO air forces became more actively involved the following spring when Operation *Deny Flight* started on 12 April 1993. As part of their significant contribution to Deny Flight, the *Armée de l'Air* deployed four Mirage F1CR photo-reconnaissance aircraft from *ER33* (*ER1/33* 'Belfort' and *ER2/33* 'Savoie') to Istrana in Italy. Their primary mission was to plot the positions of Serbian military units, especially armoured units and artillery, including those that were pounding Sarajevo, the capital of Bosnia.

The Mirage F1CRs were, typically, equipped with two MATRA 550 Magic 2s on the wingtips, Phimat chaff/flare and Barax ECM pods on the wing outer stores pylons and a Thomson-CSF ASTAC pod on the centreline station. The ASTAC pod housed an electronic reconnaissance system capable of detecting, locating and classifying hostile ground radars. The Balkans deployment also witnessed the first use of the RP35P pod (based on the 1200 litre fuel tank) by the F1CR in April 1995. This pod contained two OMERA cameras.

The next eighteen months were punctuated by a series of campaigns as all of the entities involved in the civil war sought to gain ground from their adversaries. By late October 1994, a major campaign was being fought in the north-eastern part of Bosnia-Herzegovina, around the so-called Bihac pocket and Serbian Air Force combat aircraft, in clear violation of the 'no-fly zone' were assisting their ground forces. NATO was forced to step up its air presence and eventually assembled over 350 aircraft from twelve nations in the largest coalition operation since the Gulf War some five years earlier. The *Armée de l'Air* deployed five Mirage F1CTs from *EC1/13* initially to Istrana and then subsequently to Cervia, to bolster the F1CR contingent already in theatre. In early November, NATO launched a brief bombing campaign against key Serbian targets including Udbina, a Serbian Air Base in Croatia, from where ground-attack aircraft were operating against Bosnian forces in Bihac. Both the Mirage F1CRs and F1CTs saw action – the former tasked with pre- and post-strike reconnaissance – although they occasionally carried a single 'iron' bomb for targets of opportunity in the battlefield air interdiction (BAI) role. After a brief lull in the fighting over the winter months, the warring factions commenced their summer campaigns. The August 1995 mortar attacks in Sarajevo, with considerable loss of life amongst the civilian population, provided the catalyst for NATO retaliatory attacks against Serb positions around the capital and throughout the country. Operation *Deliberate Force* took place between August and September 1995, and *Armée de l'Air* Mirages continued to play a vital role in the NATO coalition effort. In late 1995, the NATO Implementation Force (IFOR) entered Bosnia-Herzegovina to enforce the terms of the Dayton Peace Agreement between the warring factions and NATO air forces continued to maintain an air presence over the Balkans from their bases, principally located in Italy. The Mirage F1CRs, in particular, continued to provide a significant capability in their primary reconnaissance role, monitoring forces of the former warring factions on behalf of IFOR and its successor, SFOR[1].

Serbian aggression was again the cause for the next significant Mirage F1 deployment to the Balkans. In 1998, they invaded Kosovo in an attempt to stop the country becoming independent from Serbia. Fearing another humanitarian disaster on the scale of the one in Bosnia some five years earlier, NATO issued an ultimatum to Serbia to withdraw. Largely ignored, NATO launched Operation *Allied Force* in March 1999. The *Armée de l'Air* provided ten Mirage F1CTs from *EC1/30* 'Alsace' and *EC2/30* 'Normandie Niemen' to the Allied air effort. The aircraft were deployed from their base at Colmar to Istrana in northern Italy under the French codename Operation *Trident*. From April to June 1999, these aircraft conducted over seventy combat missions delivering GBU-12 Precision Guided Munitions, with the assistance of ATLIS-equipped Jaguars on strategic and high-value targets in Kosovo and Serbia, since the Mirage F1CT had yet to receive its avionics upgrade. As the NATO air campaign developed, more emphasis was placed on the need for the effective identification of tactical targets and this led to a requirement for additional aircraft in this role. France subsequently deployed eight Mirage F1CRs from *ER3/33* to Solenzara, Corsica for the remainder of the air campaign over Kosovo and former Yugoslavia. These aircraft operated with the ASTAC Elint pod, RAPHAEL SLAR and with a variety of reconnaissance pods, including RP-35P and PRESTO, providing air and ground commanders with vital information on Serbian military formations and facilities as NATO prepared for a prolonged land campaign in Kosovo and Serbia, which never actually materialised.

[1] NATO-sponsored Stabilisation Force (SFOR) empowered to conduct more 'nation rebuilding' activities once IFOR had largely implemented the peace between the former warring factions in Bosnia-Herzegovina.

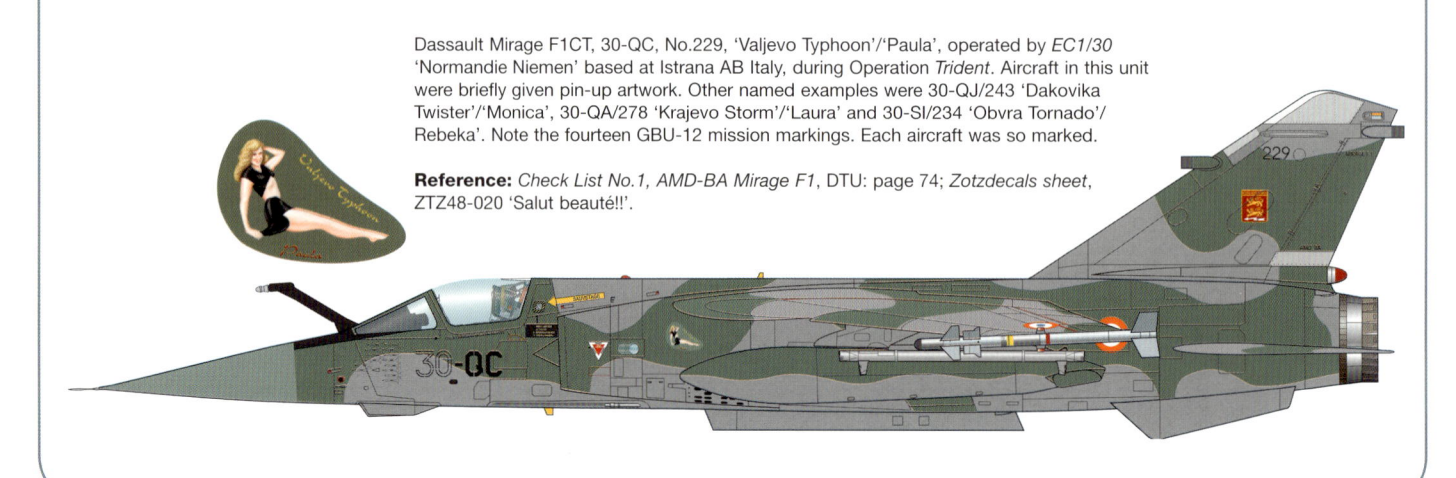

Dassault Mirage F1CT, 30-QC, No.229, 'Valjevo Typhoon'/'Paula', operated by *EC1/30* 'Normandie Niemen' based at Istrana AB Italy, during Operation *Trident*. Aircraft in this unit were briefly given pin-up artwork. Other named examples were 30-QJ/243 'Dakovika Twister'/'Monica, 30-QA/278 'Krajevo Storm'/'Laura' and 30-SI/234 'Obvra Tornado'/Rebeka'. Note the fourteen GBU-12 mission markings. Each aircraft was so marked.

Reference: Check List No.1, AMD-BA Mirage F1, DTU: page 74; *Zotzdecals sheet*, ZTZ48-020 'Salut beauté!!'.

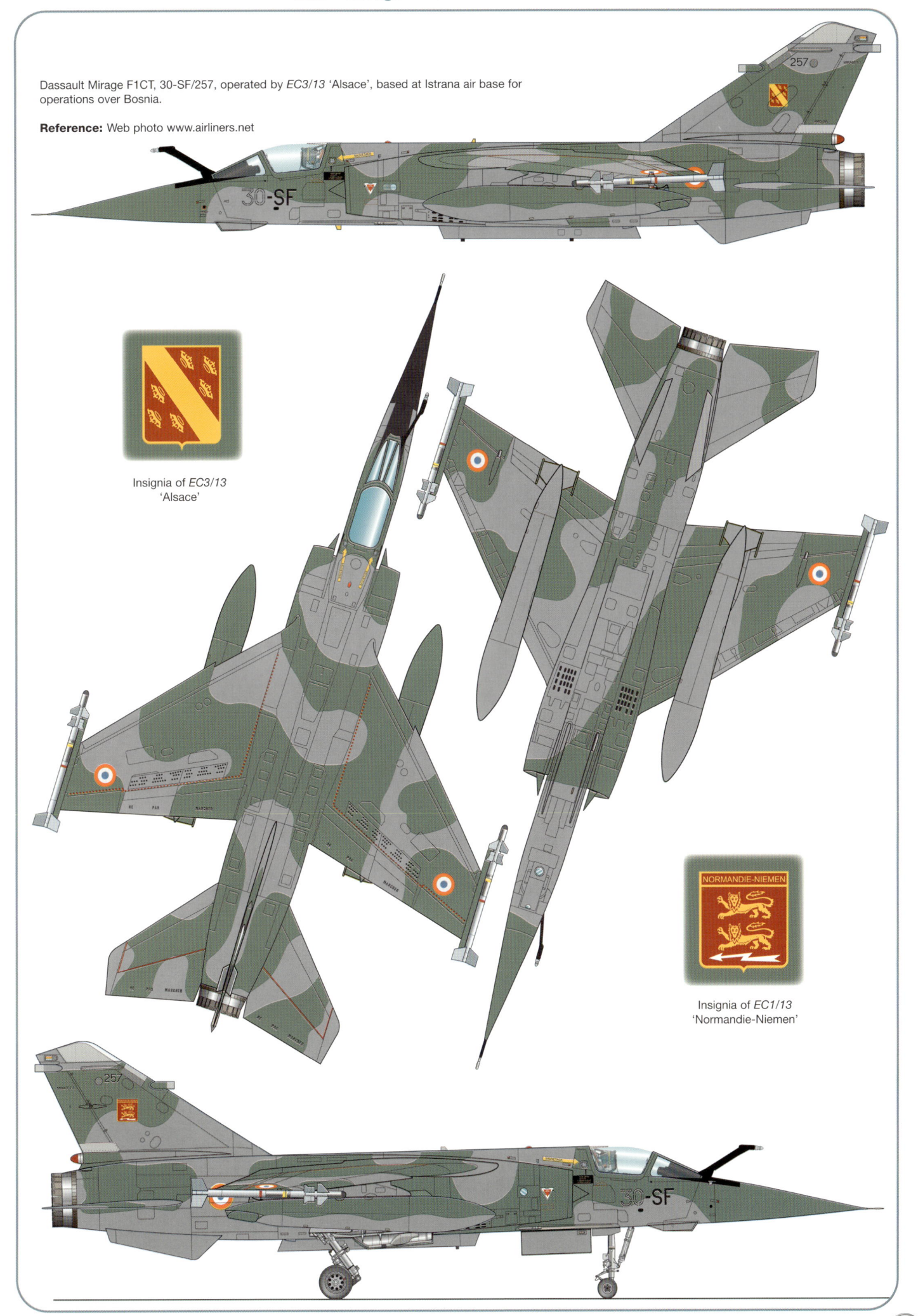

2. Mirage F1 at War – *Armée de l'Air* in the Balkans Conflict 1995–99

Dassault Mirage F1CT, 30-SF/257, operated by *EC3/13* 'Alsace', based at Istrana air base for operations over Bosnia.

Reference: Web photo www.airliners.net

Insignia of *EC3/13* 'Alsace'

Insignia of *EC1/13* 'Normandie-Niemen'

3

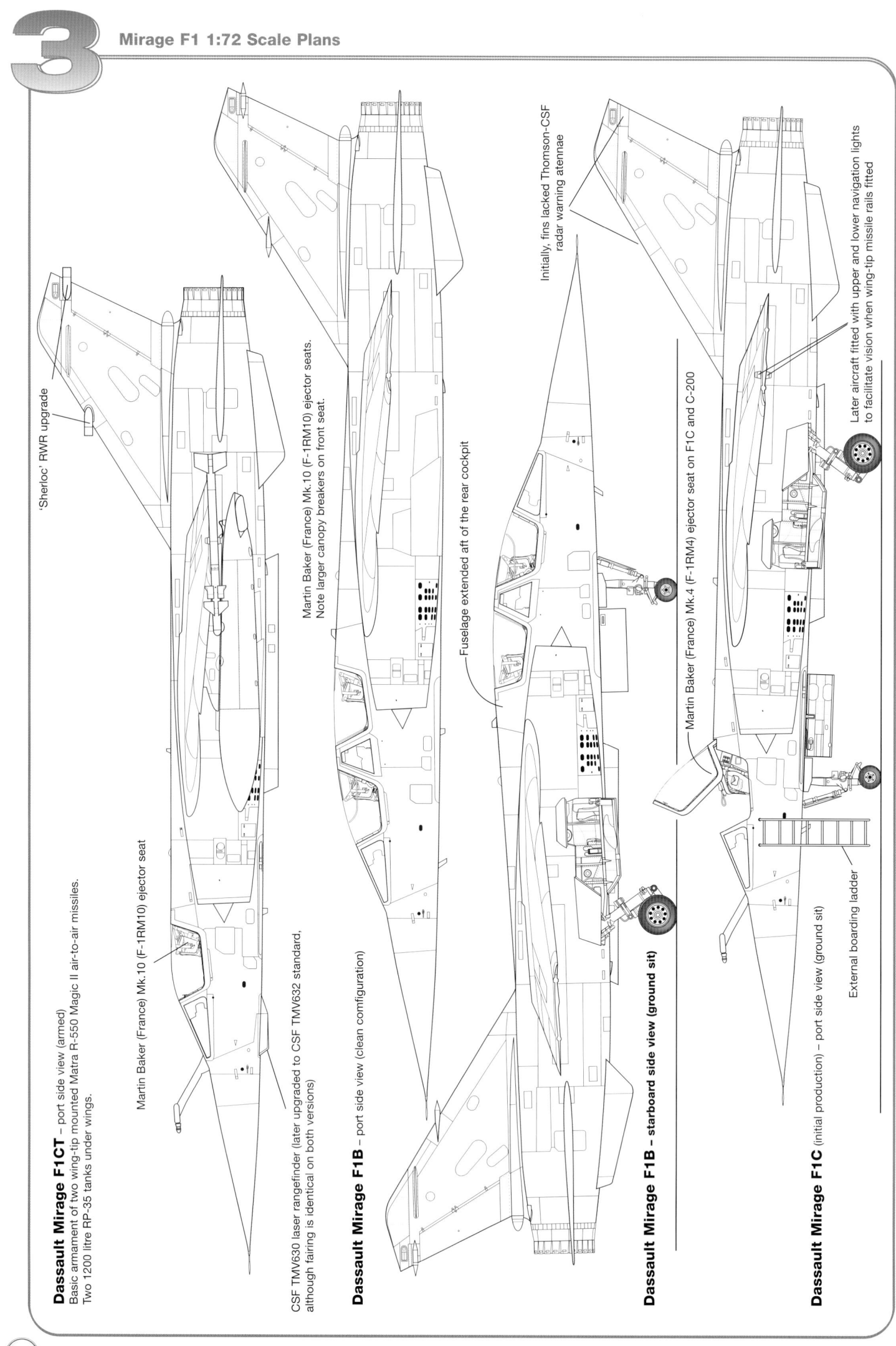

Mirage F1 1:72 Scale Plans

Initially, fins lacked Thomson-CSF radar warning atennae

Later aircraft fitted with upper and lower navigation lights to facilitate vision when wing-tip missile rails fitted

'Sherloc' RWR upgrade

Martin Baker (France) Mk.10 (F-1RM10) ejector seats. Note larger canopy breakers on front seat.

Fuselage extended aft of the rear cockpit

Martin Baker (France) Mk.4 (F-1RM4) ejector seat on F1C and C-200

Martin Baker (France) Mk.10 (F-1RM10) ejector seat

External boarding ladder

CSF TMV630 laser rangefinder (later upgraded to CSF TMV632 standard, although fairing is identical on both versions)

Dassault Mirage F1CT – port side view (armed)
Basic armament of two wing-tip mounted Matra R-550 Magic II air-to-air missiles. Two 1200 litre RP-35 tanks under wings.

Dassault Mirage F1B – port side view (clean comfiguration)

Dassault Mirage F1B – starboard side view (ground sit)

Dassault Mirage F1C (initial production) – port side view (ground sit)

44

3 Mirage F1 1:72 Scale Plans

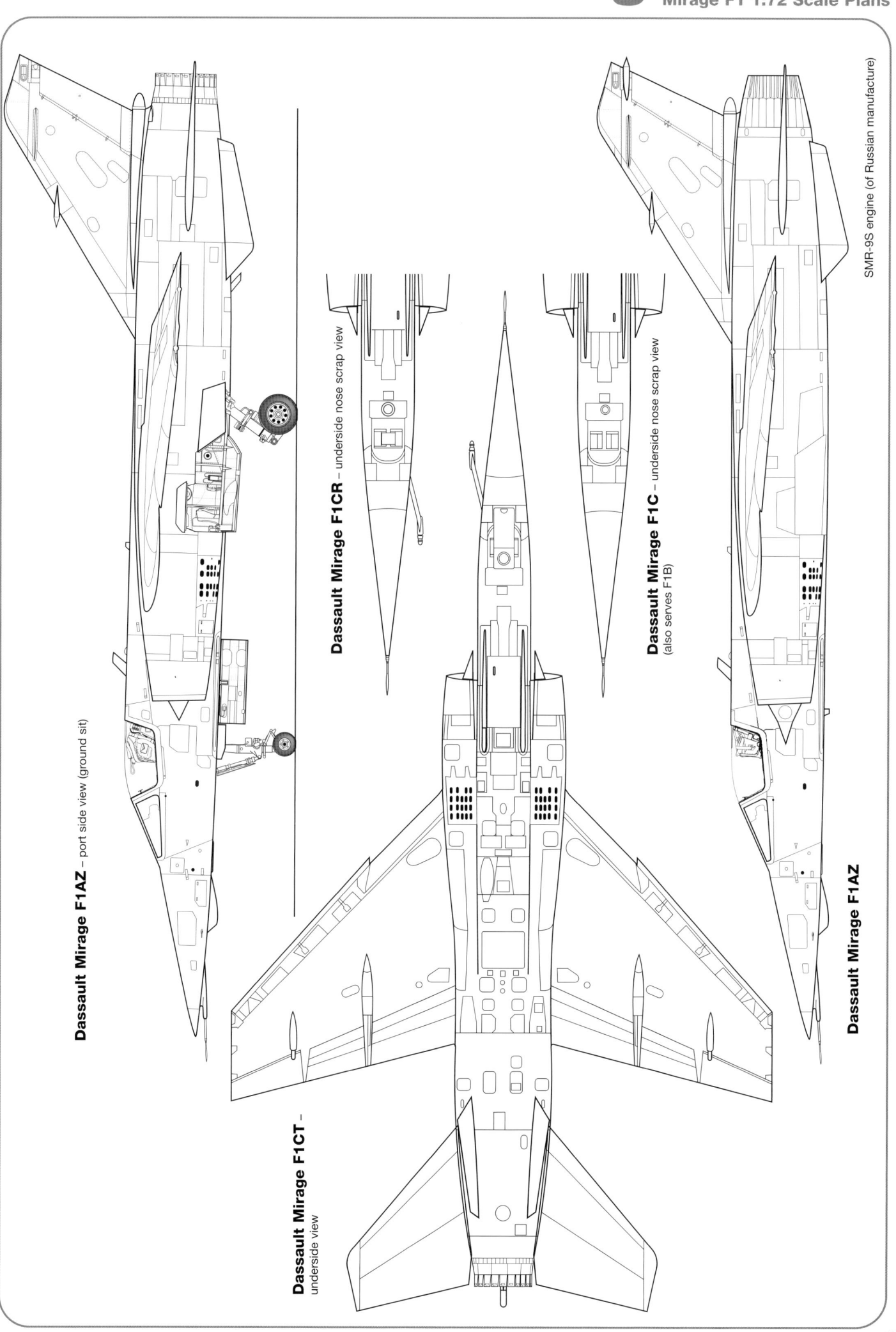

Dassault Mirage F1AZ – port side view (ground sit)

Dassault Mirage F1CT – underside view

Dassault Mirage F1CR – underside nose scrap view

Dassault Mirage F1C – underside nose scrap view (also serves F1B)

Dassault Mirage F1AZ

SMR-9S engine (of Russian manufacture)

45

3 Mirage F1 1:72 Scale Plans

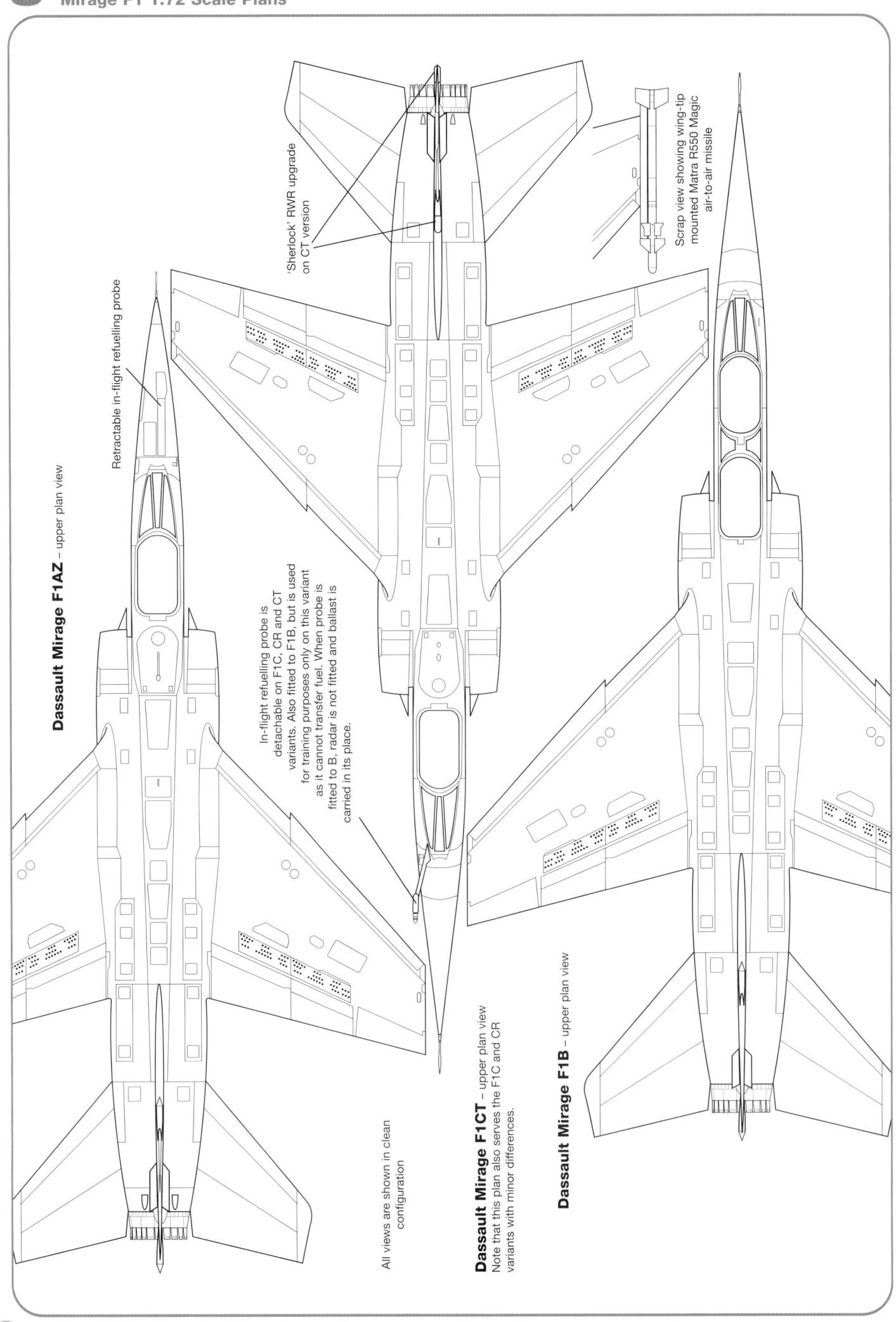

Dassault Mirage F1AZ – upper plan view

Retractable in-flight refuelling probe

'Sherlock' RWR upgrade on CT version

Scrap view showing wing-tip mounted Matra R550 Magic air-to-air missile

In-flight refuelling probe is detachable on F1C, CR and CT variants. Also fitted to F1B, but is used for training purposes only on this variant as it cannot transfer fuel. When probe is fitted to B, radar is not fitted and ballast is carried in its place.

All views are shown in clean configuration

Dassault Mirage F1CT – upper plan view
Note that this plan also serves the F1C and CR variants with minor differences.

Dassault Mirage F1B – upper plan view

46

3 Mirage F1 1:72 Scale Plans

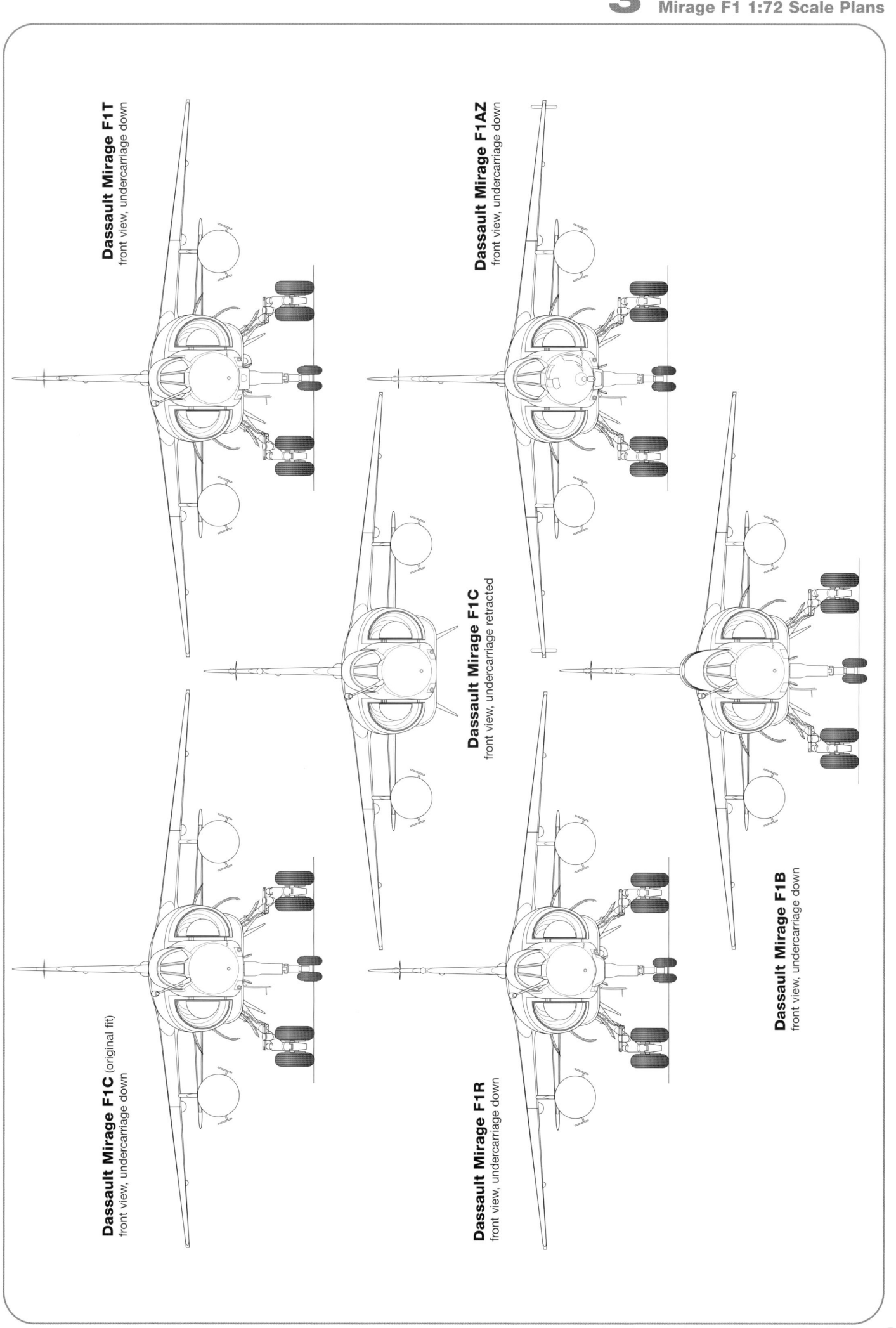

Dassault Mirage F1T
front view, undercarriage down

Dassault Mirage F1AZ
front view, undercarriage down

Dassault Mirage F1C
front view, undercarriage retracted

Dassault Mirage F1C (original fit)
front view, undercarriage down

Dassault Mirage F1R
front view, undercarriage down

Dassault Mirage F1B
front view, undercarriage down

47

3 Mirage F1 1:72 Scale Plans

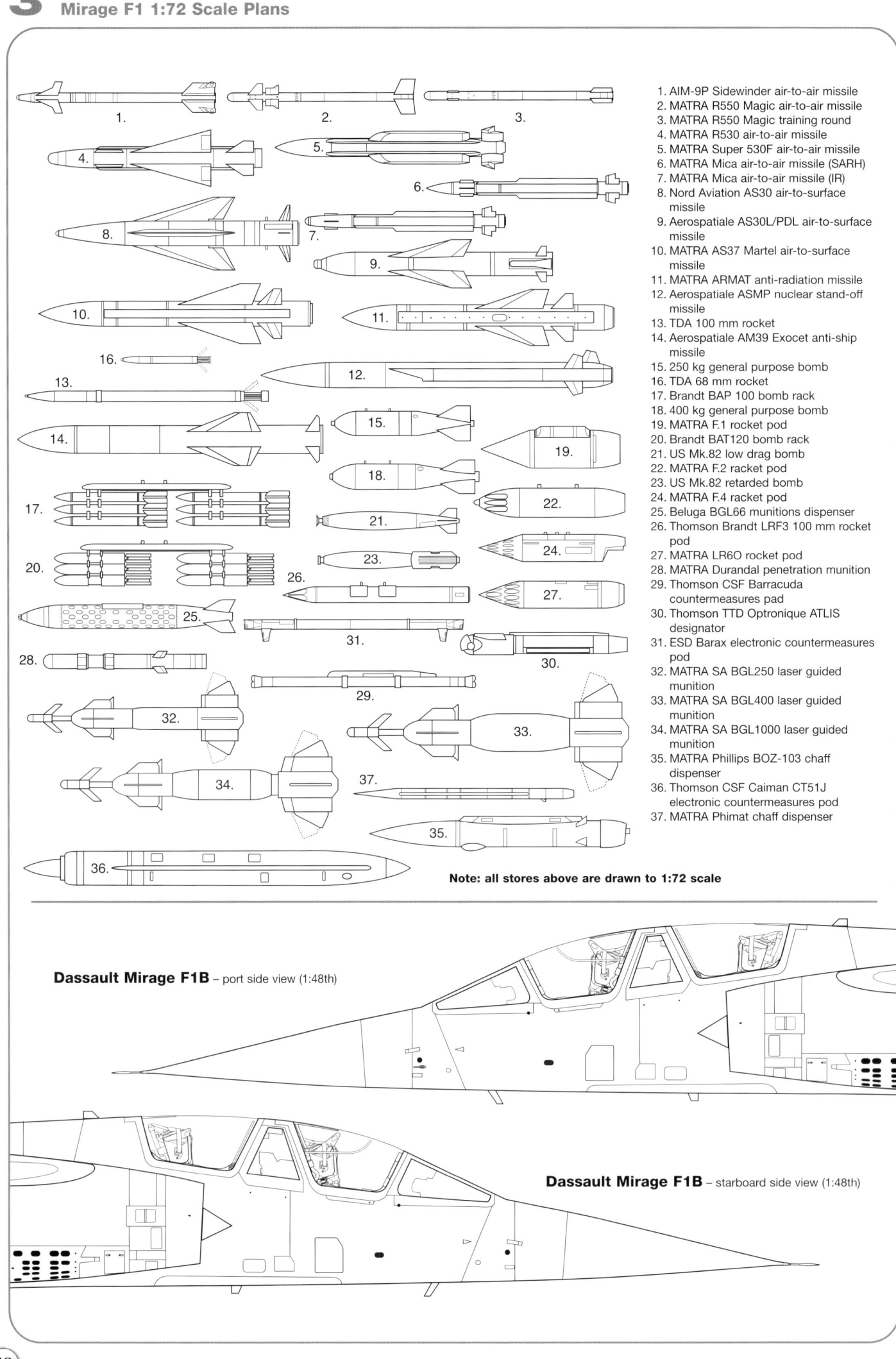

1. AIM-9P Sidewinder air-to-air missile
2. MATRA R550 Magic air-to-air missile
3. MATRA R550 Magic training round
4. MATRA R530 air-to-air missile
5. MATRA Super 530F air-to-air missile
6. MATRA Mica air-to-air missile (SARH)
7. MATRA Mica air-to-air missile (IR)
8. Nord Aviation AS30 air-to-surface missile
9. Aerospatiale AS30L/PDL air-to-surface missile
10. MATRA AS37 Martel air-to-surface missile
11. MATRA ARMAT anti-radiation missile
12. Aerospatiale ASMP nuclear stand-off missile
13. TDA 100 mm rocket
14. Aerospatiale AM39 Exocet anti-ship missile
15. 250 kg general purpose bomb
16. TDA 68 mm rocket
17. Brandt BAP 100 bomb rack
18. 400 kg general purpose bomb
19. MATRA F.1 rocket pod
20. Brandt BAT120 bomb rack
21. US Mk.82 low drag bomb
22. MATRA F.2 rocket pod
23. US Mk.82 retarded bomb
24. MATRA F.4 rocket pod
25. Beluga BGL66 munitions dispenser
26. Thomson Brandt LRF3 100 mm rocket pod
27. MATRA LR6O rocket pod
28. MATRA Durandal penetration munition
29. Thomson CSF Barracuda countermeasures pad
30. Thomson TTD Optronique ATLIS designator
31. ESD Barax electronic countermeasures pod
32. MATRA SA BGL250 laser guided munition
33. MATRA SA BGL400 laser guided munition
34. MATRA SA BGL1000 laser guided munition
35. MATRA Phillips BOZ-103 chaff dispenser
36. Thomson CSF Caiman CT51J electronic countermeasures pod
37. MATRA Phimat chaff dispenser

Note: all stores above are drawn to 1:72 scale

Dassault Mirage F1B – port side view (1:48th)

Dassault Mirage F1B – starboard side view (1:48th)

3 Mirage F1 1:48 Scale Plans

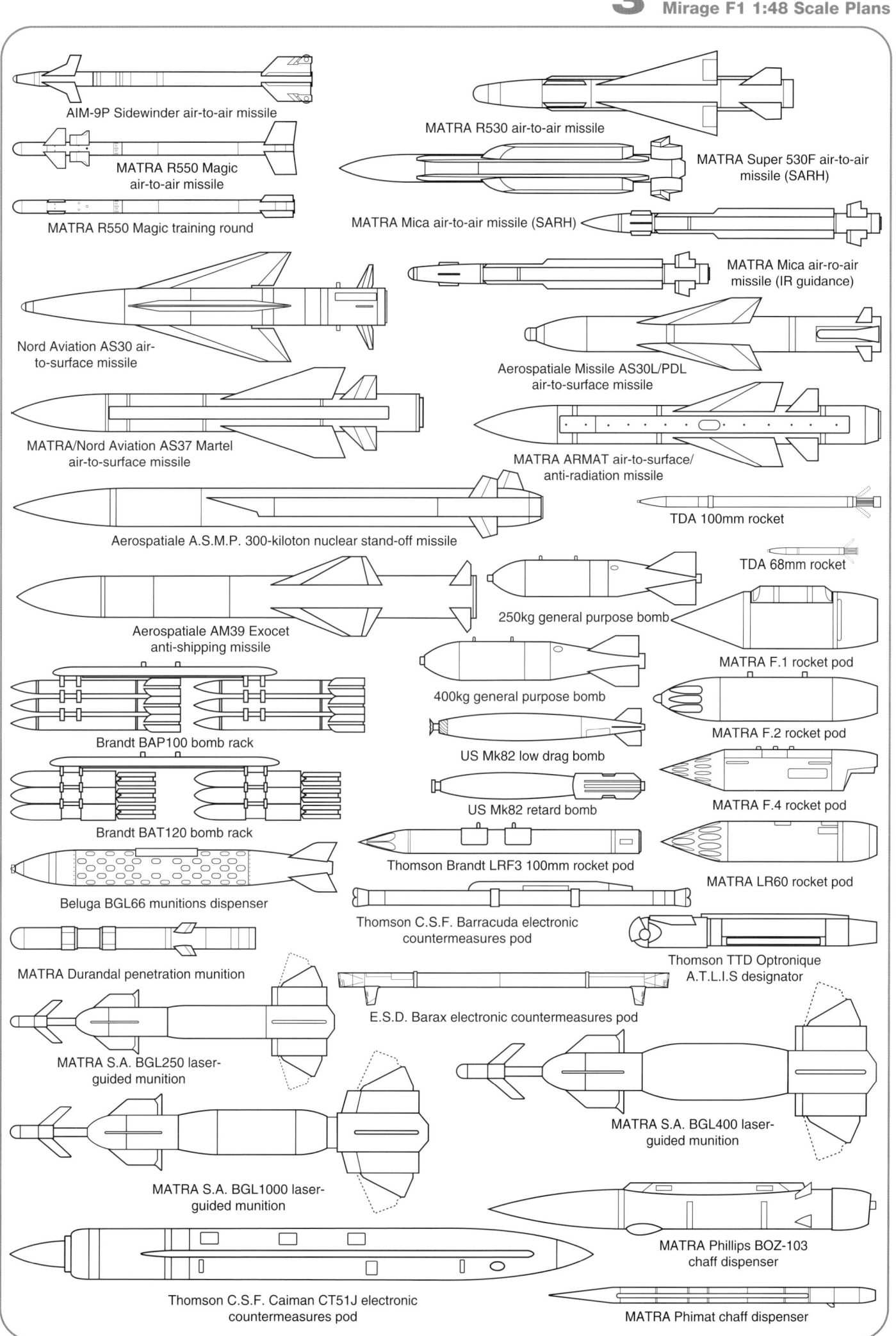

- AIM-9P Sidewinder air-to-air missile
- MATRA R550 Magic air-to-air missile
- MATRA R550 Magic training round
- MATRA R530 air-to-air missile
- MATRA Super 530F air-to-air missile (SARH)
- MATRA Mica air-to-air missile (SARH)
- MATRA Mica air-ro-air missile (IR guidance)
- Nord Aviation AS30 air-to-surface missile
- Aerospatiale Missile AS30L/PDL air-to-surface missile
- MATRA/Nord Aviation AS37 Martel air-to-surface missile
- MATRA ARMAT air-to-surface/anti-radiation missile
- Aerospatiale A.S.M.P. 300-kiloton nuclear stand-off missile
- TDA 100mm rocket
- TDA 68mm rocket
- Aerospatiale AM39 Exocet anti-shipping missile
- 250kg general purpose bomb
- MATRA F.1 rocket pod
- Brandt BAP100 bomb rack
- 400kg general purpose bomb
- MATRA F.2 rocket pod
- US Mk82 low drag bomb
- MATRA F.4 rocket pod
- Brandt BAT120 bomb rack
- US Mk82 retard bomb
- Beluga BGL66 munitions dispenser
- Thomson Brandt LRF3 100mm rocket pod
- MATRA LR60 rocket pod
- Thomson C.S.F. Barracuda electronic countermeasures pod
- Thomson TTD Optronique A.T.L.I.S designator
- MATRA Durandal penetration munition
- E.S.D. Barax electronic countermeasures pod
- MATRA S.A. BGL250 laser-guided munition
- MATRA S.A. BGL400 laser-guided munition
- MATRA S.A. BGL1000 laser-guided munition
- MATRA Phillips BOZ-103 chaff dispenser
- Thomson C.S.F. Caiman CT51J electronic countermeasures pod
- MATRA Phimat chaff dispenser

49

Mirage F1 Special Colour Schemes – NATO Tiger Meet

NATO Tiger Meet

Three units that are members of the NATO Tiger Association (NTA) have operated the Dassault Mirage F1. The first unit to convert to the type, *EC1/12* 'Cambresis', a founding member of the NTA, had previously produced some of the most spectacular colour schemes to adorn the aircraft. The unit has since re-equipped with the Dassault Mirage 2000C. Another French unit, *EC5/330* at Mont-de-Marsan still operates a number of Mirage F1s in its mixed inventory and some of the markings applied to these aircraft appear in the following pages. The third unit, *Escuadron 142* of *Ala de Caza 14* has always produced some modest tiger markings on its aircraft although in recent years these have become a little more flamboyant.

This Mirage F1B (330-AD/513) from the *Centre d'Expériences Aériennes Militaires (CEAM)* and *Escadron de Chasse 5/330* at Mont-de-Marsan had special markings applied prior to attending the 40th Anniversary NATO Tiger Meet at Kleine Brogel in Belgium in June 2001. Close-up photographs of these markings appear later in the book.

This Mirage F1CR (330-AF/605) contrasted nicely with its strike-attack colleagues at Lechfeld. Quite apart from the outlandish tiger markings, close-ups of which are included in the book, the aircraft also sports the two-tone grey/green upper camouflage scheme with silver undersurfaces. Note also the bolt-on in-flight refuelling probe and the small RWR fairings on the fin surfaces.

Mirage F1CR (330-AF/605) makes a medium level transit across southern Germany on its way to conduct another tactical reconnaissance sortie during Exercise *Clean Hunter* in June 1998.

This Dassault Mirage F.1CR of *EC5/330* appeared at the 2001 NATO Tiger Meet devoid of any special markings bar the yellow and black tiger-striped ventral strakes and centreline mounted drop tank that confirmed the unit's membership of the NATO Tiger Association.

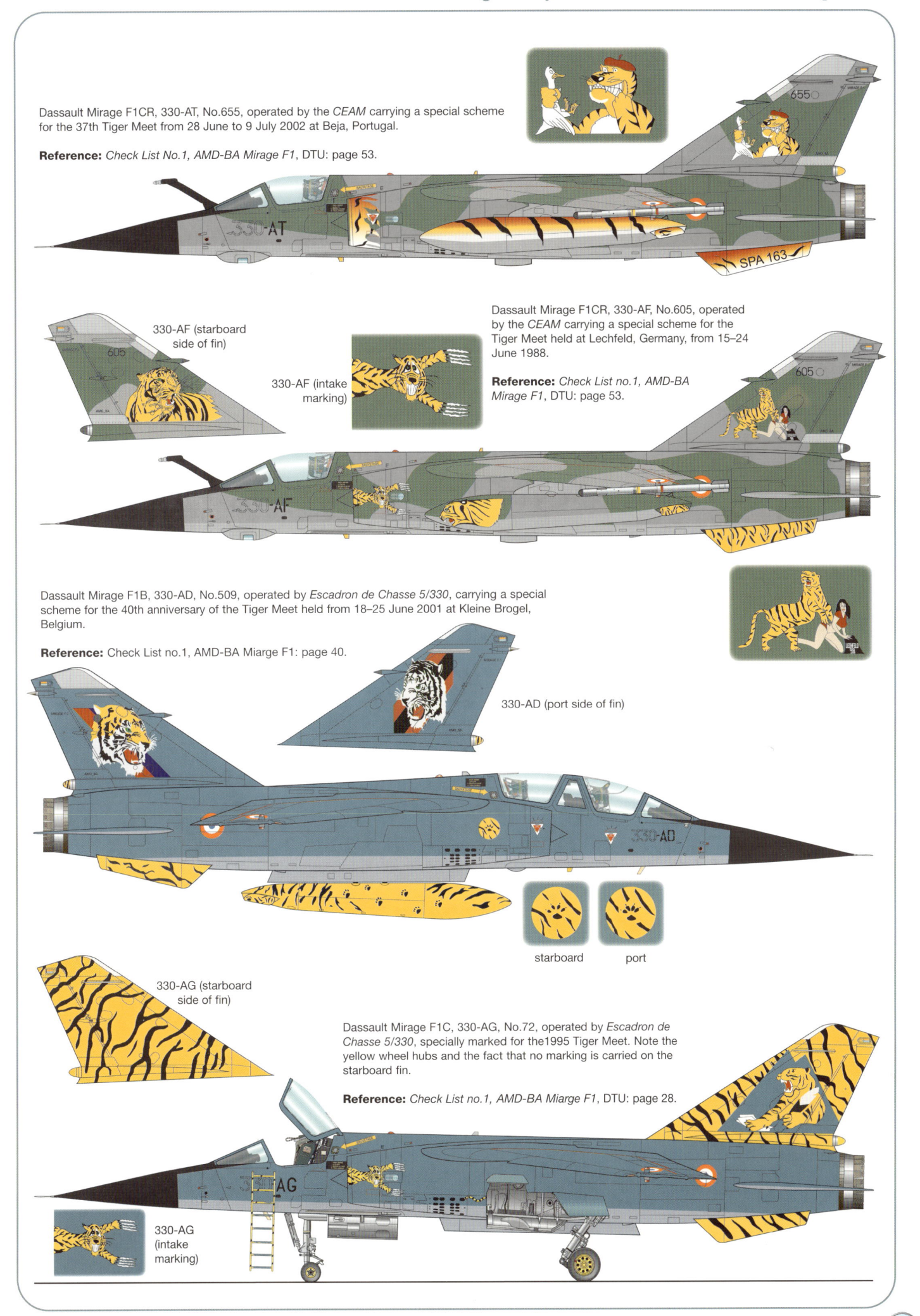

4 Mirage F1 Special Colour Schemes – NATO Tiger Meet

Dassault Mirage F1CR, 330-AT, No.655, operated by the *CEAM* carrying a special scheme for the 37th Tiger Meet from 28 June to 9 July 2002 at Beja, Portugal.

Reference: *Check List No.1, AMD-BA Mirage F1*, DTU: page 53.

Dassault Mirage F1CR, 330-AF, No.605, operated by the *CEAM* carrying a special scheme for the Tiger Meet held at Lechfeld, Germany, from 15–24 June 1988.

Reference: *Check List no.1, AMD-BA Mirage F1*, DTU: page 53.

330-AF (starboard side of fin)

330-AF (intake marking)

Dassault Mirage F1B, 330-AD, No.509, operated by *Escadron de Chasse 5/330*, carrying a special scheme for the 40th anniversary of the Tiger Meet held from 18–25 June 2001 at Kleine Brogel, Belgium.

Reference: *Check List no.1, AMD-BA Miarge F1*: page 40.

330-AD (port side of fin)

starboard   port

330-AG (starboard side of fin)

Dassault Mirage F1C, 330-AG, No.72, operated by *Escadron de Chasse 5/330*, specially marked for the 1995 Tiger Meet. Note the yellow wheel hubs and the fact that no marking is carried on the starboard fin.

Reference: *Check List no.1, AMD-BA Miarge F1*, DTU: page 28.

330-AG (intake marking)

51

4 Mirage F1 Special Colour Schemes – NATO Tiger Meet

In 2002, *EC5/330* managed to apply a host of special tiger markings to Mirage F1CR 330-AT/655 in time for the annual NATO Tiger Meet held at Beja. After a couple of days intensive flying, some of the markings started to wear off as can be seen in one or two of these views.

4 Mirage F1 Special Colour Schemes – NATO Tiger Meet

Mirage F1C, 12-YA, No.50, leased to *Escadron de Chasse 1/12* 'Cambresis' for the 1994 Tiger Meet held at that unit's home base. It should be noted that this scheme is somewhat provisional in certain areas due to incomplete reference available at the time of going to press.

Reference: *Check List No.1, AMD-BA Mirage F1*, DTU: page 27 and photographs from author's archives.

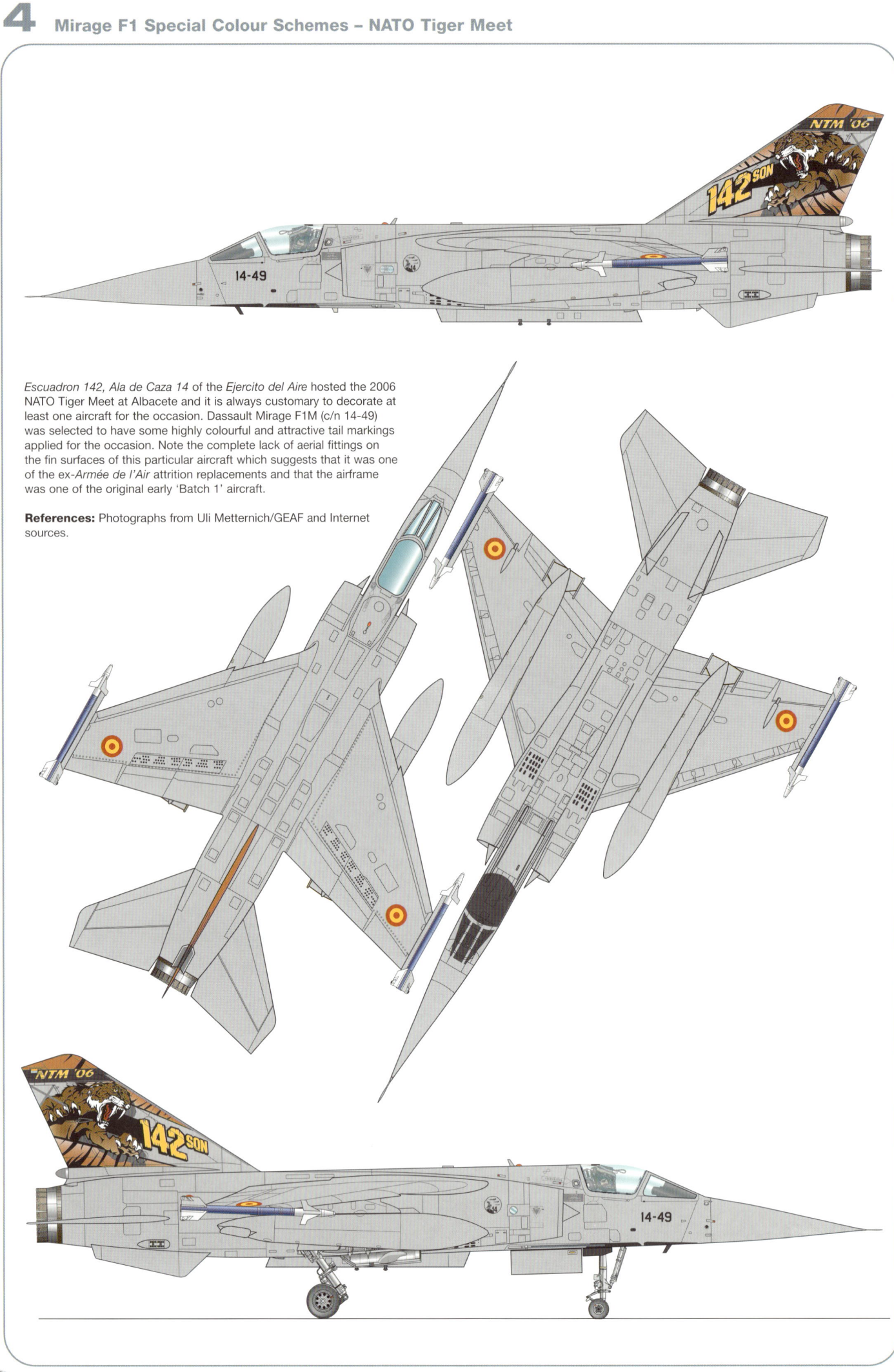

4 Mirage F1 Special Colour Schemes – NATO Tiger Meet

Escuadron 142, Ala de Caza 14 of the *Ejercito del Aire* hosted the 2006 NATO Tiger Meet at Albacete and it is always customary to decorate at least one aircraft for the occasion. Dassault Mirage F1M (c/n 14-49) was selected to have some highly colourful and attractive tail markings applied for the occasion. Note the complete lack of aerial fittings on the fin surfaces of this particular aircraft which suggests that it was one of the ex-*Armée de l'Air* attrition replacements and that the airframe was one of the original early 'Batch 1' aircraft.

References: Photographs from Uli Metternich/GEAF and Internet sources.

4 Mirage F1 Special Colour Schemes – NATO Tiger Meet

Escuadron 142, Ala de Caza 14 of the *Ejercito del Aire* hosted the 2006 NATO Tiger Meet at Albacete and it is always customary to decorate at least one aircraft for the event. On this occasion, the Spanish unit decorated two aircraft in highly distinctive special markings.

Dassault Mirage F1M (c/n 14-37/C-14-64) was nicely presented with low-visibility tiger stripes on the rear fuselage, fin and upper wing surfaces.

Dassault Mirage F1M (c/n 14-49) wore high-visibility tail markings which contrasted nicely with the overall light grey air-defence colour scheme. Note the complete lack of aerial fittings on the fin surfaces of this particular aircraft. (Photos: Uli Metternich/GEAF (2) and Jim Smithe 'Air Press Photos')

55

4 Mirage F1 Special Colour Schemes – *Armée de l'Air*

Armée de l'Air

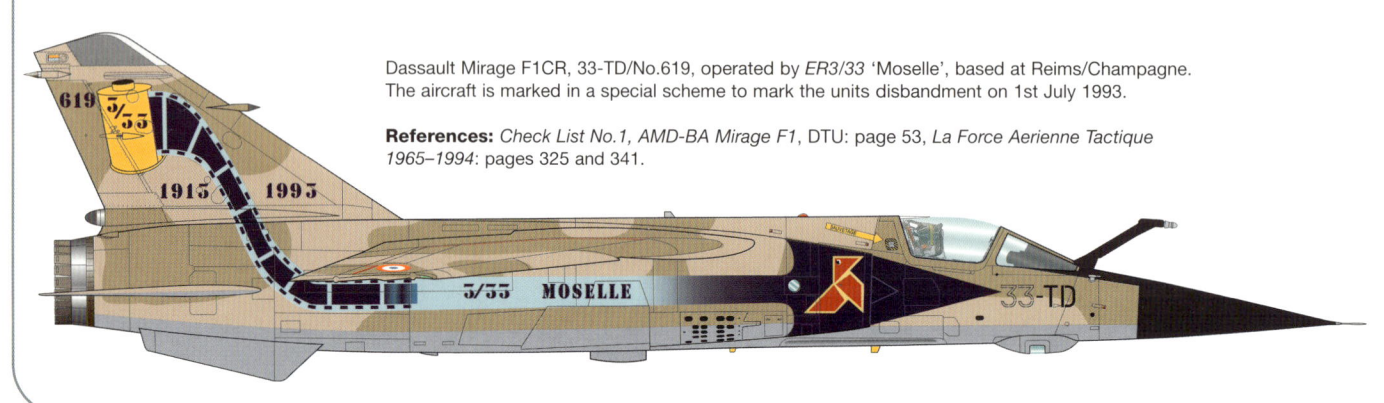

To celebrate the units ninetieth anniversary, *ER11* painted up F1CR, 33-NJ in this simple but very attractive scheme. Various aircraft type silhouettes used throughout *ER11*'s history were applied to the side of the fuselage. The units 'Cocotte' (Paper Bird) insignia adorned the fin. (Photo: via Aviation Workshop Photo Archive)

Another beautiful ninety years scheme, this time *ER 1/33* 'Belforts' Mirage F1CR, 33-CB of *SAL 33*. Like 33-NJ, the unit had applied historical silhouettes to the fuselage, with the large 'Hache d'Abordage' (Boarding Axe) covering the fin. (Photo: via Aviation Workshop Photo Archive)

Finally, 33-NH of *SAL 6* adorned again in a commemorative ninety years scheme, resplendent with aircraft silhouettes and the units 'Mouette du Rhin' (Rhine Gull) applied to the fin and rear fuselage. (Photo: via Aviation Workshop Photo Archive)

Dassault Mirage F1CR, 33-TD/No.619, operated by *ER3/33* 'Moselle', based at Reims/Champagne. The aircraft is marked in a special scheme to mark the units disbandment on 1st July 1993.

References: *Check List No.1, AMD-BA Mirage F1, DTU*: page 53, *La Force Aerienne Tactique 1965–1994*: pages 325 and 341.

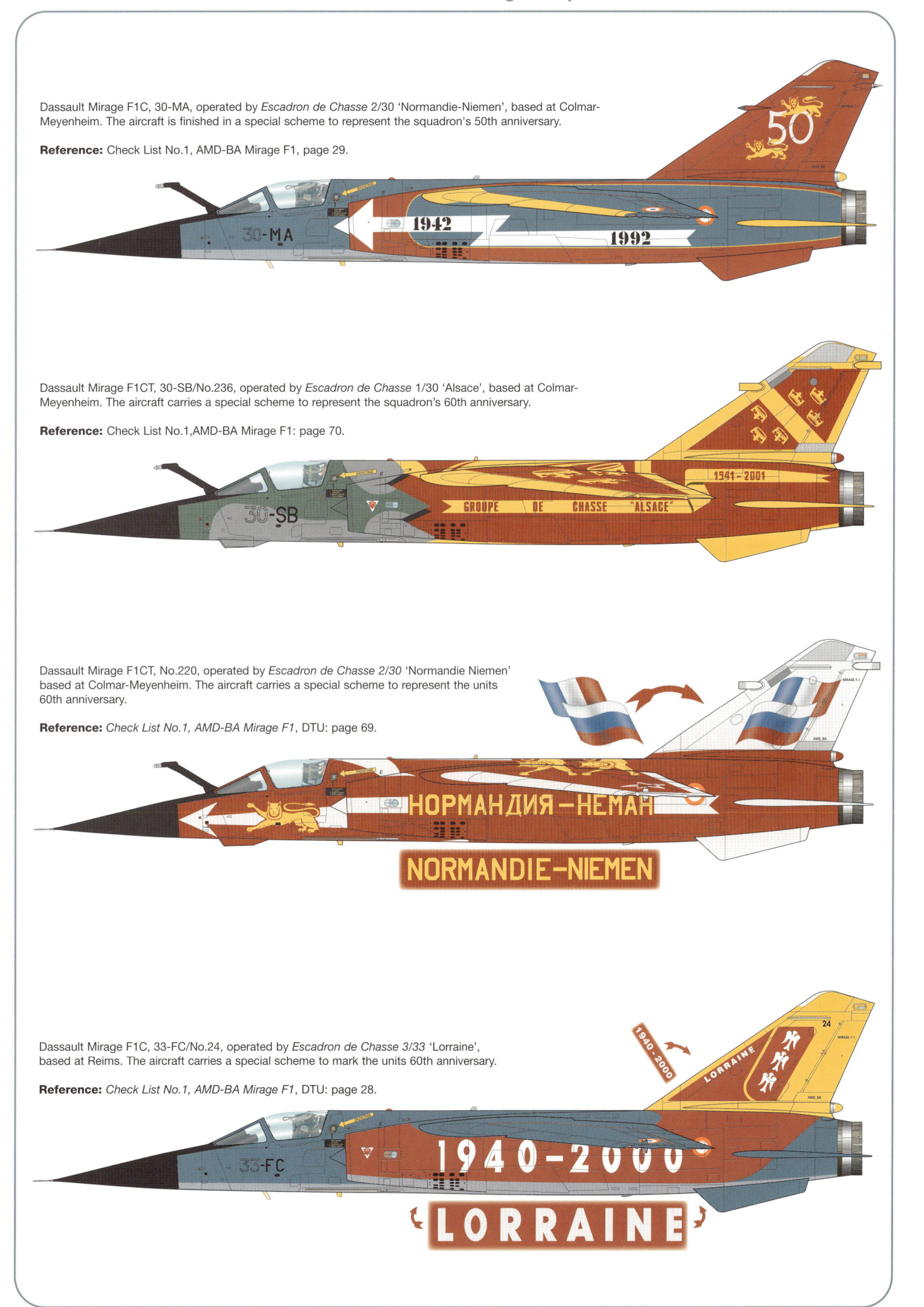

4 Mirage F1 Special Colour Schemes – *Armée de l'Air*

Dassault Mirage F1C, 30-MA, operated by *Escadron de Chasse 2/30* 'Normandie-Niemen', based at Colmar-Meyenheim. The aircraft is finished in a special scheme to represent the squadron's 50th anniversary.

Reference: Check List No.1, AMD-BA Mirage F1, page 29.

Dassault Mirage F1CT, 30-SB/No.236, operated by *Escadron de Chasse 1/30* 'Alsace', based at Colmar-Meyenheim. The aircraft carries a special scheme to represent the squadron's 60th anniversary.

Reference: Check List No.1, AMD-BA Mirage F1: page 70.

Dassault Mirage F1CT, No.220, operated by *Escadron de Chasse 2/30* 'Normandie Niemen' based at Colmar-Meyenheim. The aircraft carries a special scheme to represent the units 60th anniversary.

Reference: *Check List No.1, AMD-BA Mirage F1*, DTU: page 69.

Dassault Mirage F1C, 33-FC/No.24, operated by *Escadron de Chasse 3/33* 'Lorraine', based at Reims. The aircraft carries a special scheme to mark the units 60th anniversary.

Reference: *Check List No.1, AMD-BA Mirage F1*, DTU: page 28.

4 Mirage F1 Special Colour Schemes – *Armée de l'Air*

Dassault Mirage F1CR, 33-NG/No.608, operated by *Escadron de Reconnaissance 2/33* 'Savoie' based at Reims. This aircraft wore a very striking red and white commemorative colour scheme with unit titles and squadron heraldry, including the famous 'Rhine Gull' and 'Paper Bird' insignia on the upper surfaces.

Reference: web photos from www.airliners.net

58

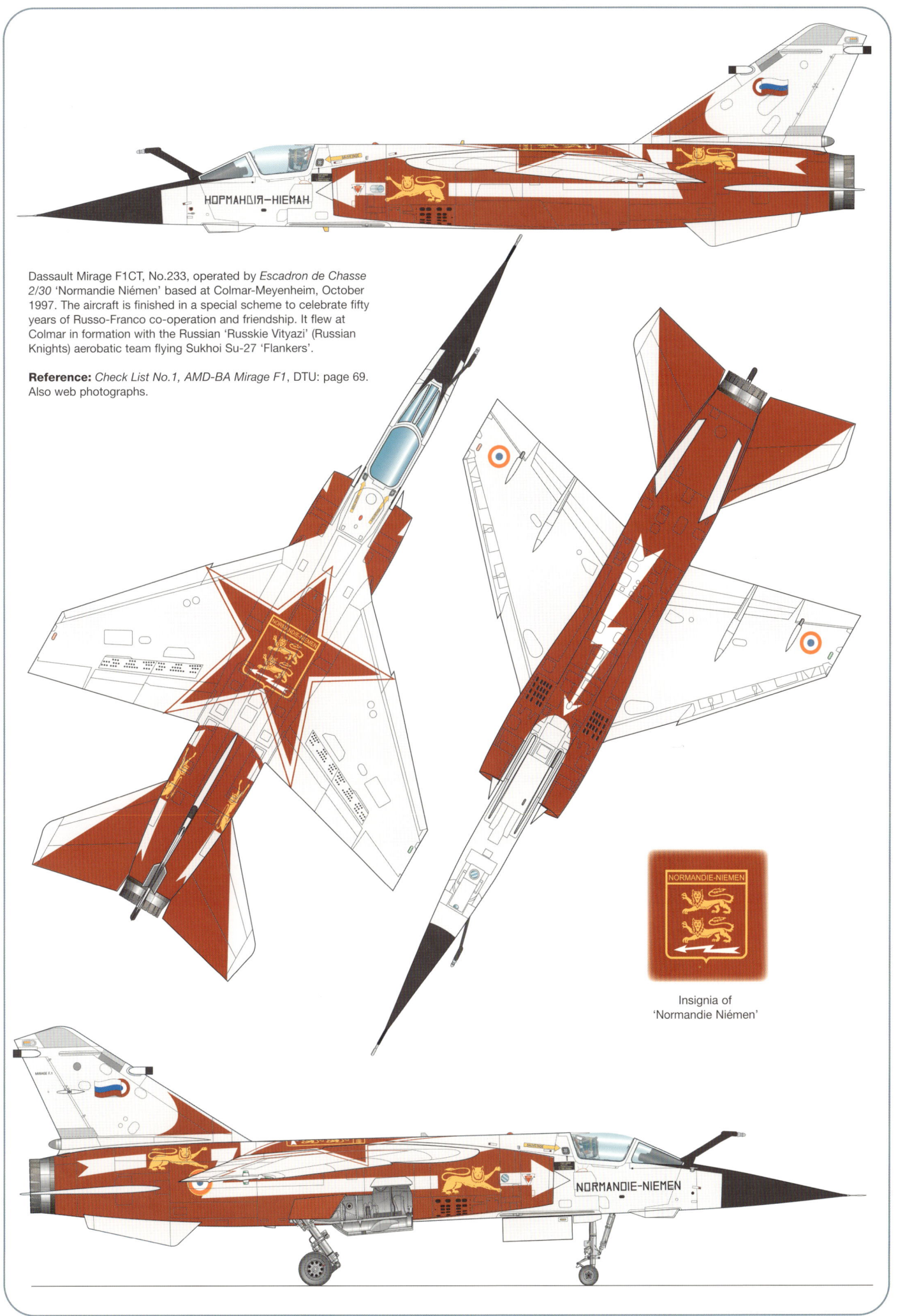

4 Mirage F1 Special Colour Schemes – *Armée de l'Air*

Dassault Mirage F1CT, No.233, operated by *Escadron de Chasse 2/30* 'Normandie Niémen' based at Colmar-Meyenheim, October 1997. The aircraft is finished in a special scheme to celebrate fifty years of Russo-Franco co-operation and friendship. It flew at Colmar in formation with the Russian 'Russkie Vityazi' (Russian Knights) aerobatic team flying Sukhoi Su-27 'Flankers'.

Reference: *Check List No.1, AMD-BA Mirage F1*, DTU: page 69. Also web photographs.

Insignia of 'Normandie Niémen'

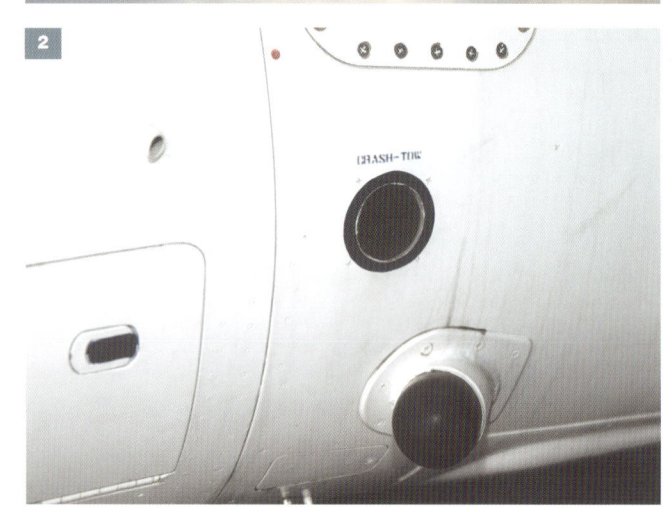

5

Mirage F1 In Detail – South African Mirage F1AZ/CZ

1. One of the most notable features of the F1A variant is the nose radome. The rearrangement of avionics equipment in the nose of the F1A version necessitated the relocation of the pitot probe from the tip, on the original radome, to a fairing on the undersurfaces as can be clearly seen here.

2. This close-up shot of the port forward fuselage shows one of the modifications common to all SAAF Mirage F1AZs. A total of four RWR fairings, colloquially referred to as 'Cats Balls', were located either side of the forward fuselage and as a pair on the leading edge of the upper fin surfaces.

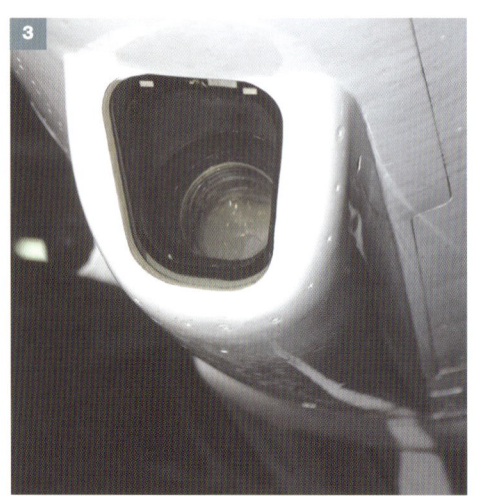

3. Close-up of the housing for the Thomson CSF TMV-630 laser range finder synonymous with the ground-attack role of the F1AZ.

4. A useful close-up of the windscreen framing. Note the small rain dispersal nozzle at the base of the flat windscreen section.

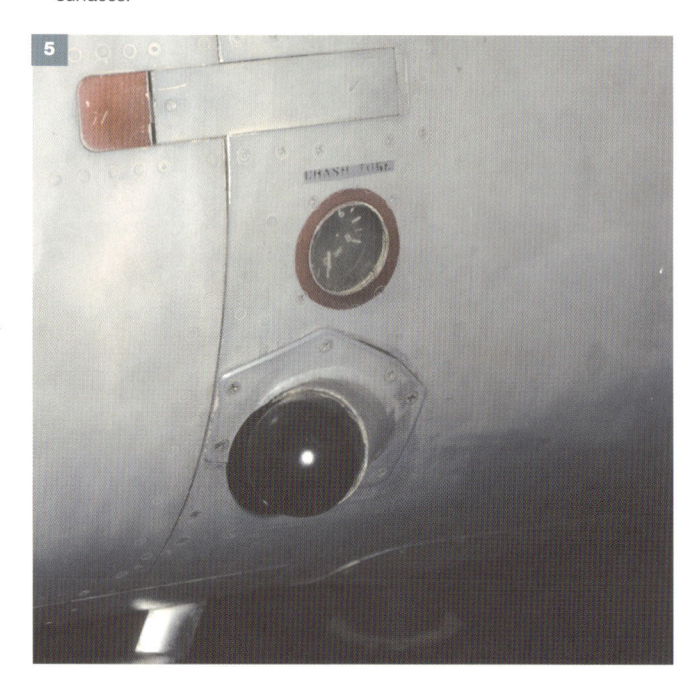

5. View of the port forward fuselage area, showing the prominent fairing for the 'Cats Ball' ECM sensor, which was fitted to all SAAF F1s.

6. This probe appears on the lower fuselage surfaces adjacent to the hinge line for the nose radome.

7. Close-up view of the dynamic pressure sensor located just below the windscreen on the starboard side of the forward fuselage.

5 Mirage F1 In Detail – South African Mirage F1AZ/CZ

1 This round fairing, located under the nose radome forward of the nose undercarriage appears to be peculiar to the SAAF F1CZ variant. Note also the dummy canopy markings, applied in Matt Black, designed to disorientate adversaries during air-to-air combat.

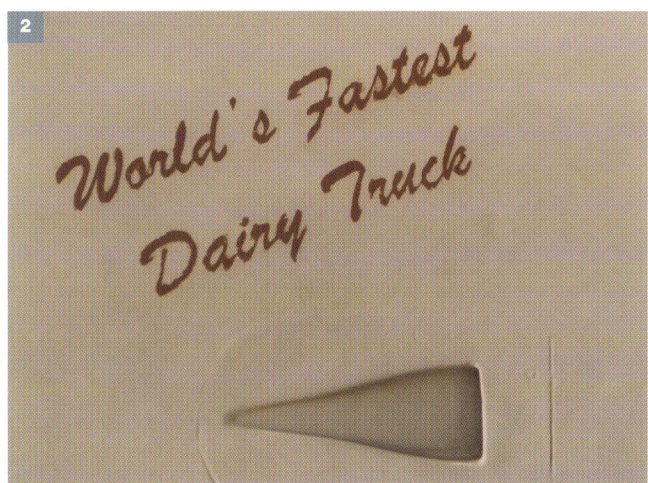

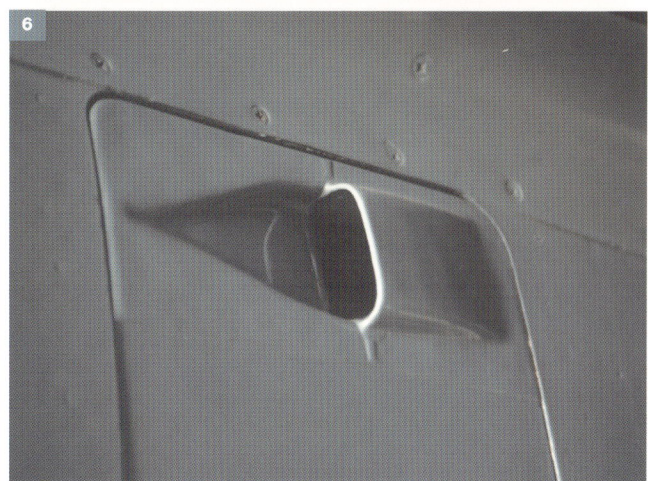

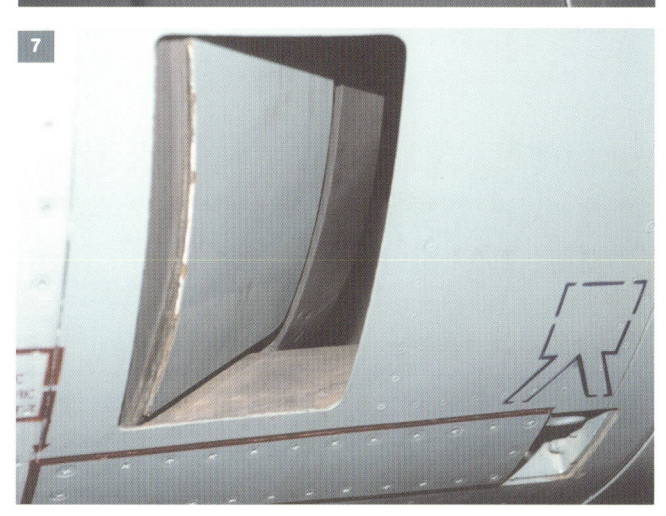

2 Close-up of the 'World's Fastest Dairy Truck' logo that appears on the port forward fuselage below the windscreen. Note the small intake.

3 Useful close-up photograph of the port air intake. The contrasting colour scheme helps to distinguish some of the detail that is not easily discernible with the more effective camouflage schemes applied to these combat aircraft.

4 Unusual view of the upper surfaces of the port air intake which shows the position of the various bracing struts.

5 A general view of the forward fuselage and cockpit area of Dassault Mirage F1AZ serial '235'. Note the traditional style for the titles beneath the cockpit.

6 Close-up shot of the intake that appears on the upper port fuselage immediately underneath the leading edge of the mainplane.

7 This intake suction relief door, shown in the open position, is located on the lower port air intake just behind and below the SAAF national markings.

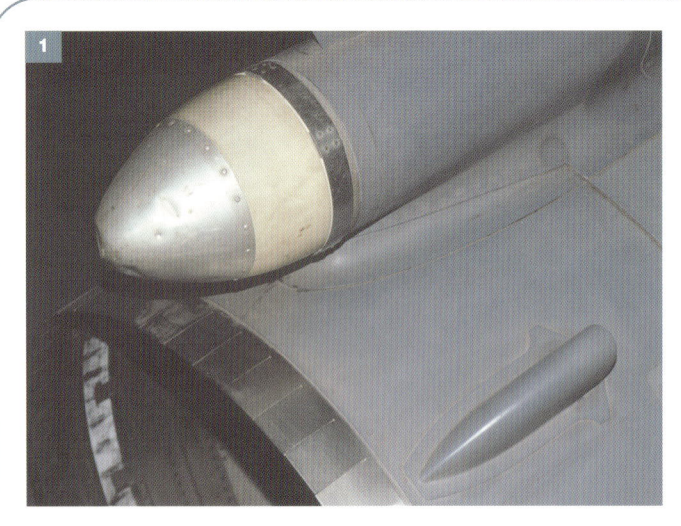

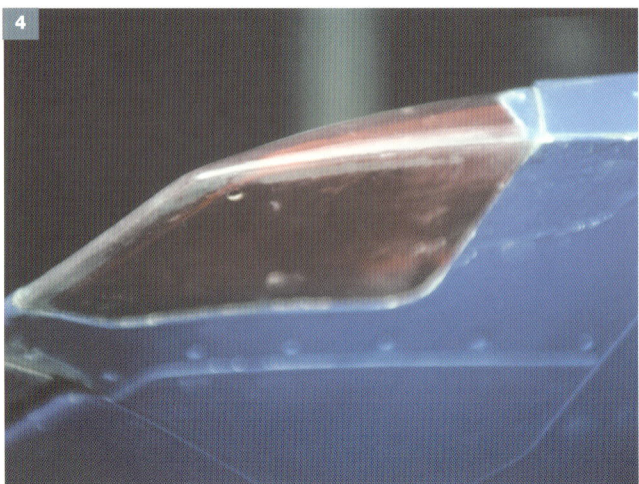

5 Mirage F1 In Detail – South African Mirage F1AZ/CZ

1 Close-up of the rear fuselage showing the brake parachute housing and the small air intake fairing that is located at the base of the fin.

2 The starboard fin surfaces, which highlight the arrangement of the various RWR antenna fairings on this particular variant, including the paired 'Cats Balls' on the upper leading edge surfaces. Note also the well-worn low-visibility camouflage scheme and the oversprayed insiginia of No.3 Squadron.

3 Close-up of the 'Cats Balls' RWR fairing located on the upper leading edge of the fin surfaces on Mirage F1CZ '203'.

4 Close-up of the navigation light mounted in the leading edge of the port wingtip. This particular part of the Mirage F1 airframe is not always discernible since it is often 'hidden' behind a wing-tip mounted launch rail for missiles.

5 A rather empty extreme rear fuselage area of '235'. In keeping with standard SAAF policy for static exhibits at the SAAF museum at Swartkop, the SNECMA Atar 09K50 turbojet engine has been removed from the airframe. Note also the absence of the fairing 'bullet' at the base of the fin/rudder.

6 View of the lower mainplane surfaces clearly showing the shape of one of the main flying surface actuator fairings.

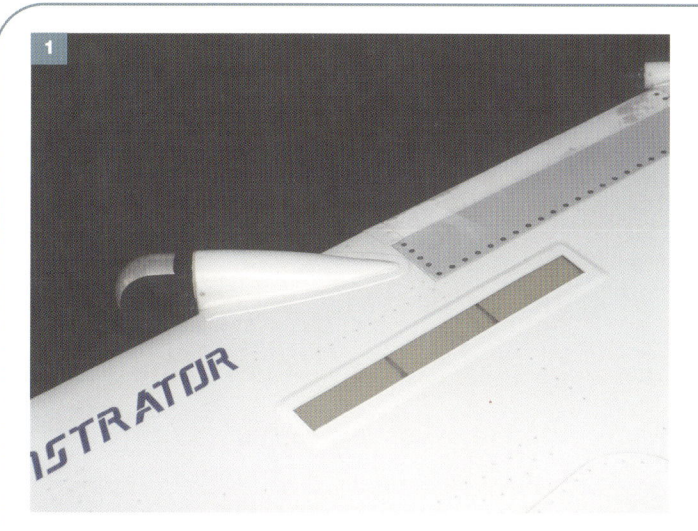

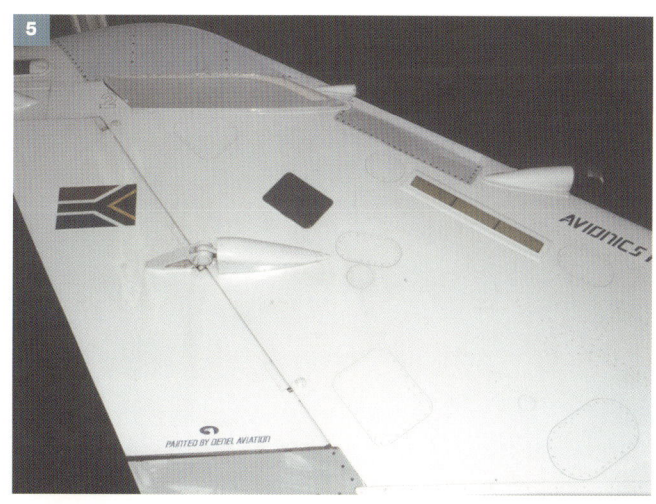

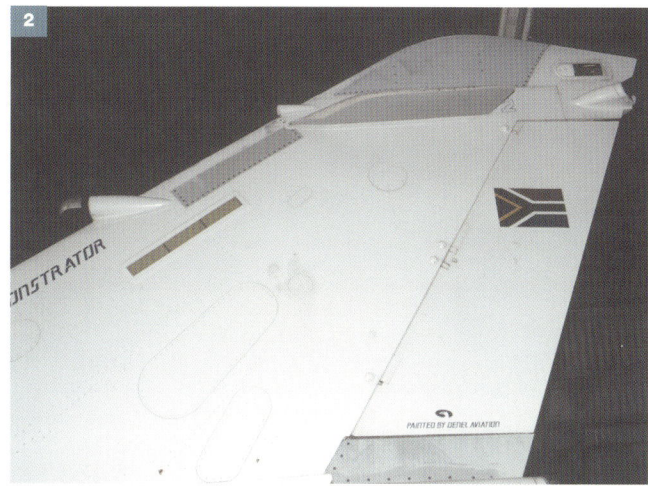

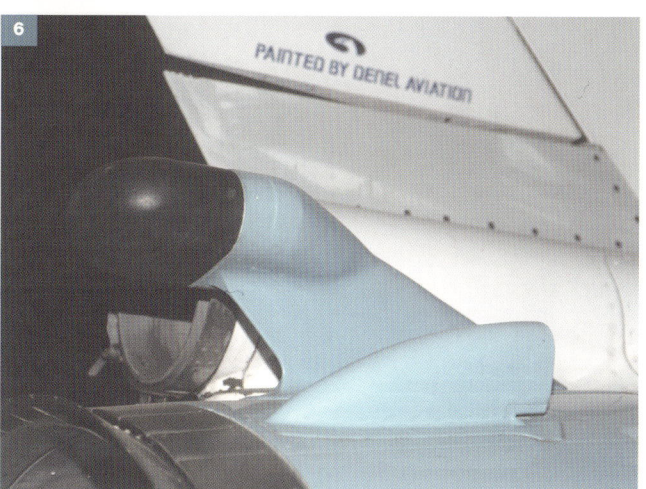

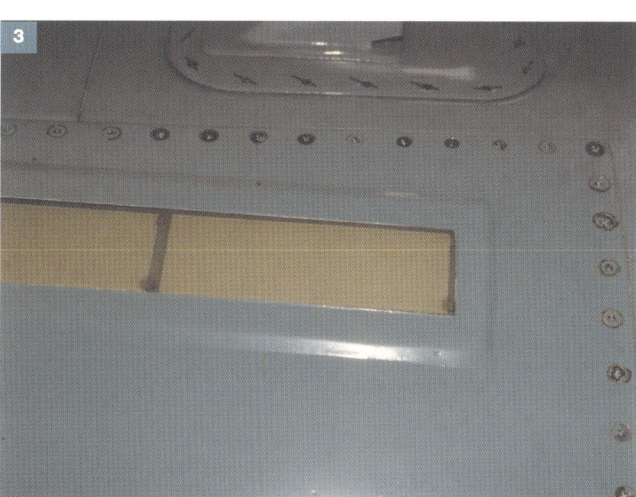

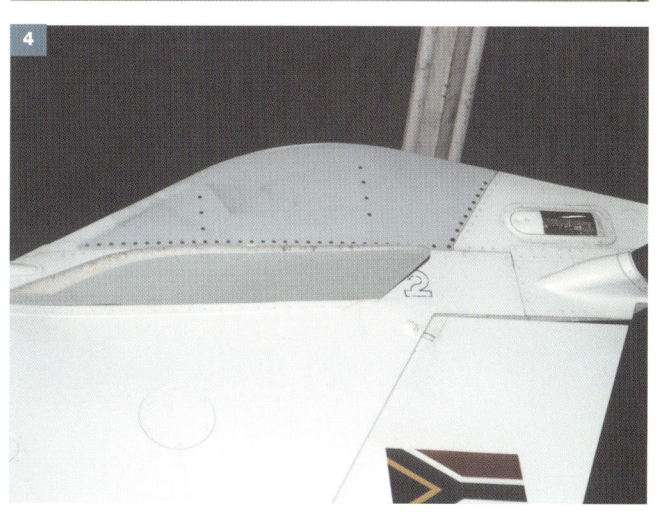

5 Mirage F1 In Detail – South African Mirage F1AZ/CZ

1 The fin area of '235' has clearly been subjected to a range of modifications including this fairing, probably housing RWR equipment, which was mounted half way down the leading edge of the fin. Note also the position of the fin-mounted 'slime' navigation strip.

2 General view of the port fin surfaces, showing the position of the national flag on the rudder and the 'Avionics Flight Demonstrator' titles, in black, along the forward fin area.

3 Upper starboard rear fuselage area, showing the small intake that is located midway along the base of the fin and a section of one of the 'slime' navigation strip lights fitted to the rear fuselage of '235' as part of the upgrade programme.

4 Close-up of the upper port fin surfaces, showing the standard VOR aerial fins and the 'Cats Balls' RWR fairings mounted on the leading edge of the fin.

5 General view of the starboard fin surfaces.

6 View of the upper starboard fuselage area, immediately adjacent to the rear base of the fin, showing another avionics fairing and one of the standard auxiliary air intakes. The fairing would appear to house yet another variety of electronic Defensive Aids Suite (DAS).

7 Upper rear port fuselage area showing one of the auxiliary air intakes, this time from the front.

63

5 Mirage F1 In Detail – South African Mirage F1AZ/CZ

1 The starboard upper wing surfaces, showing the distinctive perforated spoiler panels and the wing-tip missile launch rail with an Armscor V3B Kukri missile (indigenous version of the MATRA R.550 Magic missile) fitted. Note also the well-worn 'Ghost' camouflage pattern and the full-colour 'castle' insignia, which appear to have largely escaped the effects of the overspraying that was applied to the fuselage area.

2 Close-up of the old-style 'castle' markings in Blue with a White outline and the 'Springbok' insignia applied to SAAF aircraft prior to 1994.

3 Close-up of one of the two-segment double slotted flaps and the perforated spoiler panels. Note the red warning stripe and 'No Step' markings applied in Afrikaans.

4 Port wing surfaces showing the spoiler panel and the slightly different pattern of camouflage demarcation between the Mirage and Highveld Grey shades to that found on the Starboard wing surfaces of '203'.

5 Close-up of the leading-edge flap showing the prominent 'dog-tooth'.

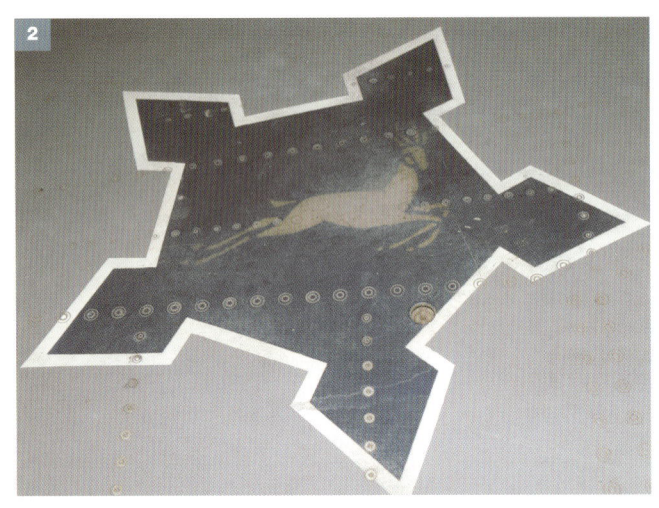

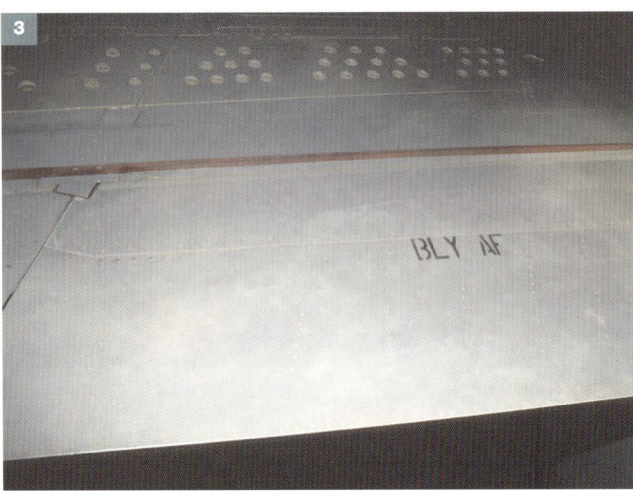

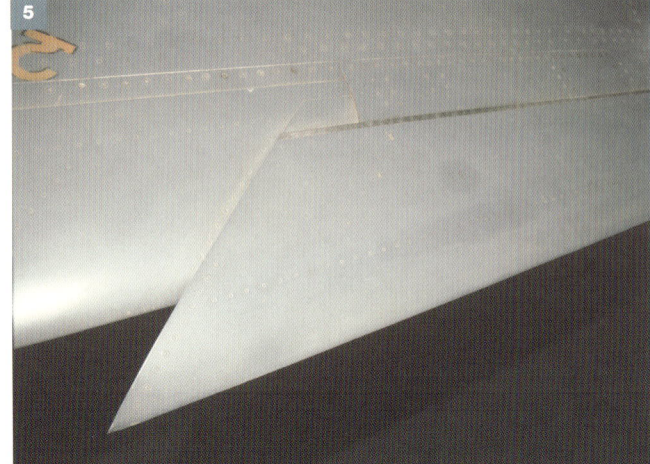

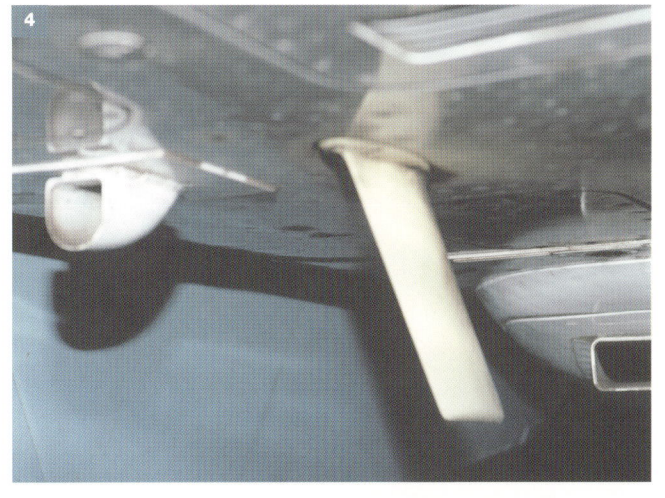

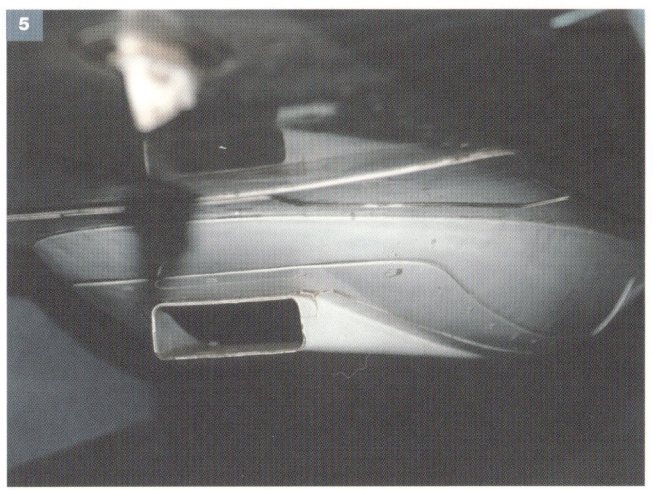

5 Mirage F1 In Detail – South African Mirage F1AZ/CZ

1. Port rear fuselage, showing the serial number and a pair of fuel dump pipes mounted on the lower fuselage just above the leading edge of the ventral strake.

2. A single dump pipe, this time mounted on the starboard lower fuselage adjacent to the ventral strake.

3. Close-up view which shows the plethora of intakes, fairings and grilles that occupy the central fuselage area between the main undercarriage.

4. View of the small intake fairing and blade aerial that are mounted on the lower fuselage in line with the leading edges of the ventral strakes. Both appear to be common to the F1AZ variant and not just to '235'.

5. This large intake fairing, mounted on the lower rear fuselage of '235' between the ventral strakes, is a very interesting modification which is peculiar to this aircraft and one other modified F1AZ in SAAF service. It is probably part of the cooling system for the vast array of new avionics systems fitted to the aircraft.

6. View of the upper fuselage area, immediately behind the cockpit which provides some useful detail, including the shape and position of the blade aerial fitted to the F1AZ variant and one of the 'slime' navigation strips fitted to '235' as part of her modification programme.

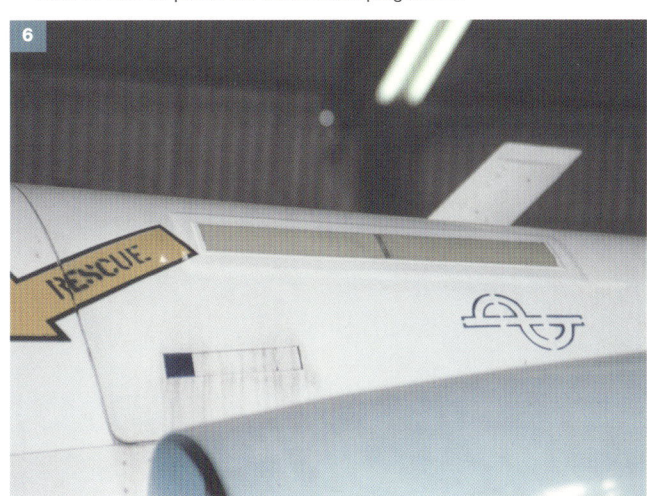

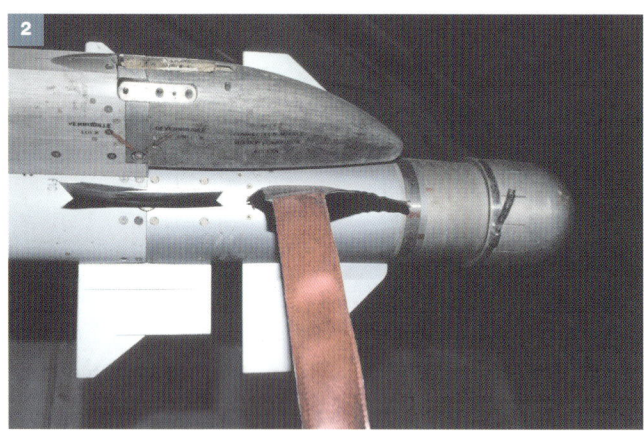

5 Mirage F1 In Detail – South African Mirage F1AZ/CZ

1. Undersurfaces of the port wing-tip showing the mounting fairings for the missile rail and the navigation light.
2. Close-up of the front section of the wingtip missile launch rail and an inert drill V3B Kukri missile round.
3. A useful close-up shot of the starboard airbrake door. Once again the bright colour scheme on '235' helps to distinguish the shape and style of the apertures found on the doors, a key feature of the Mirage F1.
4. General view of the cockpit windscreen. This Mirage F1CZ carries the name of Major Johann Venter, the last pilot to be assigned to this particular aircraft, rather than that of the pilot that gained the Angolan 'kill' marking applied lower on the forward fuselage.
5. This general view of the instrument panel show the dominance of the overall Satin-Black colour scheme and the rubber 'boot' that covers the radar display. Note also the right hand cockpit console, which can also be partially seen.
6. The left hand cockpit console, which houses a number of controls and switches, including those for the engine and the radio/communication suite.
7. Lower section of the Martin-Baker Mk.4 ejection seat fitted to this Mirage F1CZ. Note the different shading of the various seat and lumbar support cushions and the Bronze and Blue-coloured lap straps and harness. The ejection seat frame was originally Gloss Black although this has taken on a satin sheen with use.
8. Upper portion of the Martin-Baker Mk.4 ejection seat, showing the prominent Black and Yellow activation handle and some useful references for the cockpit bulkhead area immediately behind the seat.

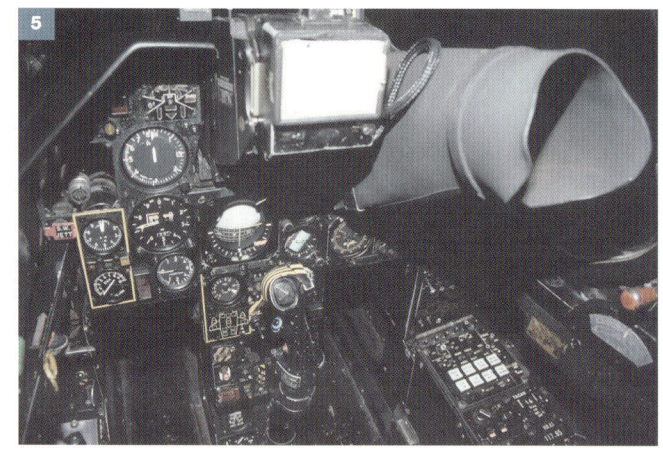

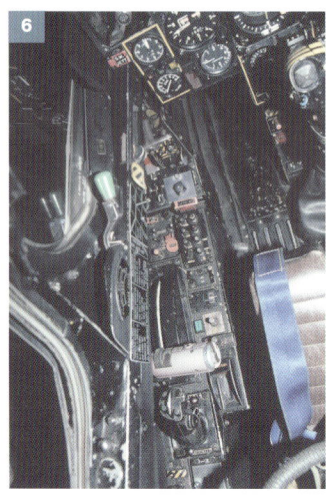

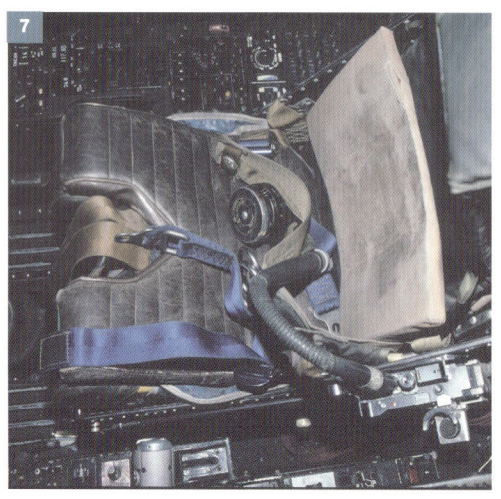

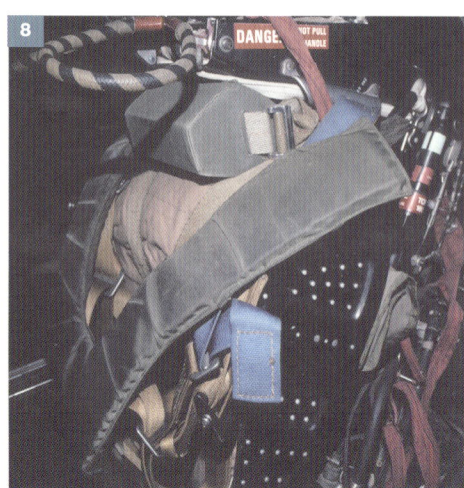

5 Mirage F1 In Detail – Spanish Mirage F1M

1 Forward fuselage details of a Spanish Mirage F1. Note the single adjustable taxi-light, which is located in the port intake cheek and the various rescue and warning markings including the red 'collar' around the leading edge of the air intake. The *14 Ala de Caza* (Wing) badge, also carried on the air intakes, shows the legendary Spanish character, Don Quixote, saluting a flight of Mirage F1s.

2 View of the mainplane undersurfaces clearly showing the position of the inboard stores pylon and the actuator fairings.

3 Close-up of the undersurfaces of the main stores pylon.

4 View of the lower mainplane surfaces clearly showing the shape of one of the main flying surface actuator fairings.

5 Upper fin of a Spanish F1M showing the VOR antenna and rear-facing RWR fairing on the fin trailing edge. Note the low visibility Spanish Air Force markings.

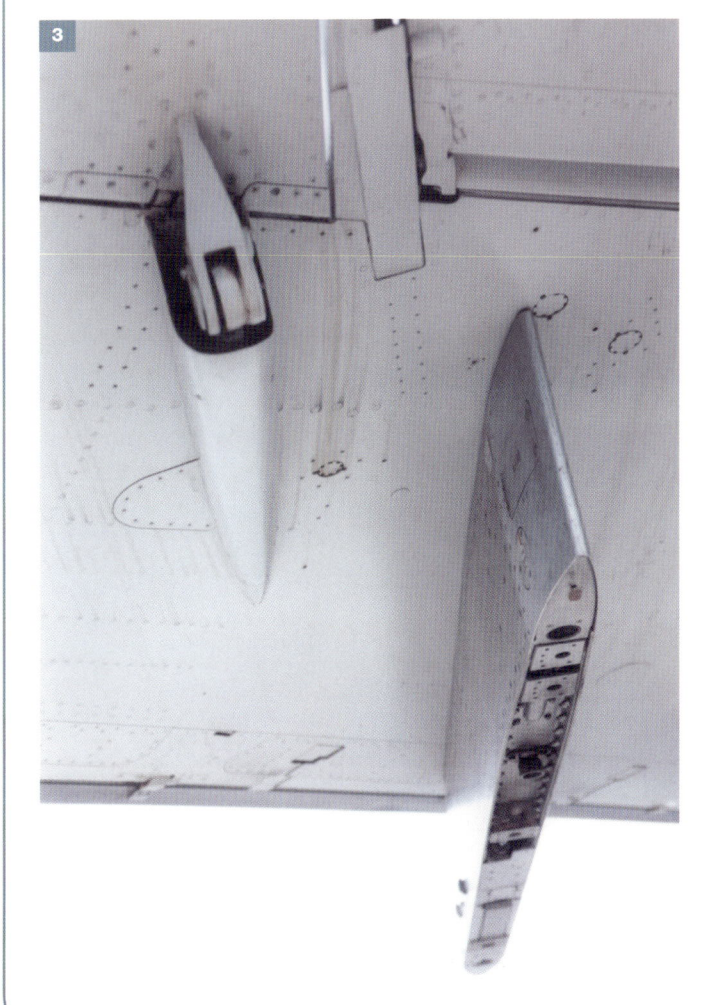

67

5   Mirage F1 In Detail – Spanish Mirage F1M

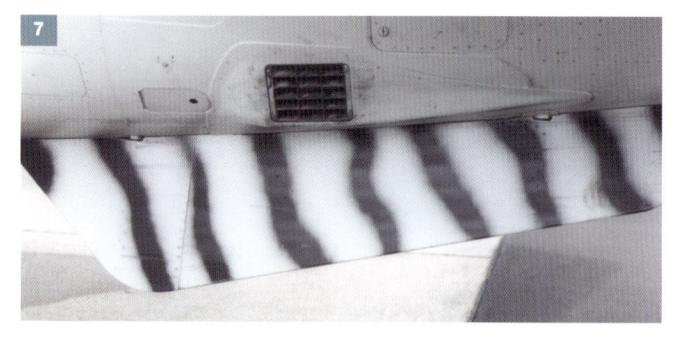

1/2 Two views of the bolt-on in-flight refuelling probe, which has been optional equipment on all versions of the F1 from the -200 series onwards, including the F1EE seen here. The only exceptions have been the Libyan and South African F1As which were equipped with a retractable IFR probe in the nose radome. Note also the position of the dynamic pressure sensor.

3/4 In keeping with the majority of Mirage F1 variants, *Ejercito del Aire* aircraft are equipped with a pair of 30 mm DEFA 553 cannons in the lower forward intake trunking. These close-up photographs clearly show the design of the gun barrel and trough that runs along the bottom of the forward fuselage. Note also the shape of the underfuselage air intake and the navigation light.

5 Close-up of the light fairing found on the outer wall of the Port air intake fairing.

6 The Mirage F1 is powered by a single SNECMA Atar 9K-50 engine. This view clearly shows the variable area afterburner nozzle.

7 Ventral strake on a Spanish F1M, which on this occasion has been tiger-striped for participation in a NATO Tiger Meet. Note the shape and location of the chaff fairings fitted to *Ejercito del Aire* aircraft.

5 Mirage F1 In Detail – Spanish Mirage F1M

4/5 Two close-up views of the starboard air intake area. The first shows, in particular, the retractable landing light, which differs considerably from the arrangement found on the port intake. Note the small blade antenna that appears on the nose undercarriage door. The two images also show the access door for the safety switch box, which has been left open during a routine turnaround of the aircraft. Mounted on the inside of the door is the 'key' for opening the canopy when the aircraft is static and a maintenance manual has also been stowed in the bay.

6 Cockpit canopy in the open position. Many of the markings shown are common to the majority of Mirage F1s, regardless of which air arm they serve. In general, only the language will differ although low visibility versions are now appearing in line with a general move towards toned-down markings.

1 General view of the nose undercarriage leg, doors and wheels. Note the silver finish, which is common to almost all Mirage F1 variants in service.

2 This unusual view shows the rear of the nose undercarriage leg/wheel assembly. This provides valuable reference for the arrangement of the brake and hydraulic pipes on the rearmost section of the leg. Note also the various indentations on the inner surfaces of the main undercarriage door, to the right of the picture and the gun trough, upper left of the view.

3 Interior detail on the main nose undercarriage door, finished in silver.

69

5 Mirage F1 In Detail – Spanish Mirage F1M

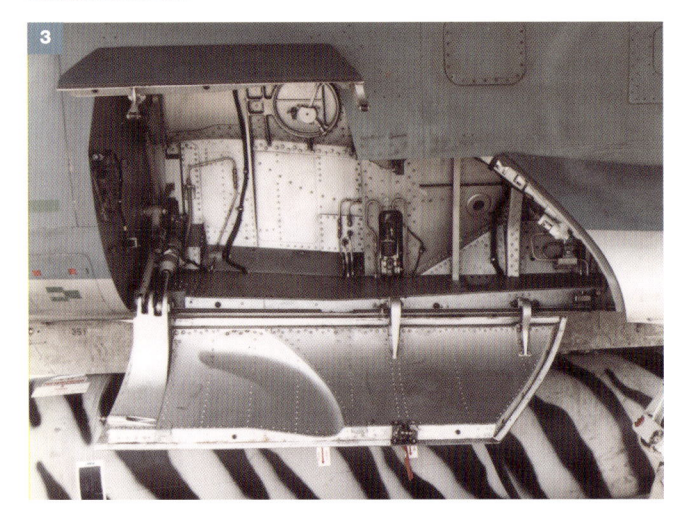

1–4 This series of four classic 'walkaround' shots clearly shows the arrangement of the main undercarriage and bay assembly as well as some useful references for the centreline stores pylon, drop tank and air brake doors. A quick scan of photographs of the Mirage F1 at rest, including some contained in this book, suggests that there is no set arrangement for the main undercarriage doors when the aircraft is at rest. Some views show aircraft with the main undercarriage doors closed whilst others reveal them as fully deployed. On this occasion the *Ejercito del Aire* obliged the photographer by leaving the doors in the deployed position so the modeller has access to some valuable reference material on the interior surfaces of the undercarriage bays. Other items of note are the complexity of the main undercarriage leg assembly, the demarcation line between the upper and undersurface colour scheme and the various green markings denoting the 'function' of the various panels adjacent to the main undercarriage bay.

5 Views of the starboard main undercarriage bay, showing the door assemblies and the slightly different arrangement of pipework and other fittings on the interior surfaces.

6/7 Close-up views of the main Messier-Hispano-Bugatti undercarriage leg and wheels, showing clear signs of in-service wear on the leg strut and rotating linkage arm. The rather awkward looking undercarriage arrangement, reminiscent of that found on the SEPECAT Jaguar, was designed to allow the aircraft to operate from austere or semi-prepared surfaces.

70

5 Mirage F1 In Detail – Spanish Mirage F1M

1 View of the upper left-hand side of the main instrument panel.

2 Left-hand instrument console and ejection seat details.

3 Right-hand instrument console. This view also shows the cockpit sill to good effect

4 An excellent general view of the main instrument panel in the upgraded Mirage F1M showing some of the multi-function displays and the control column.

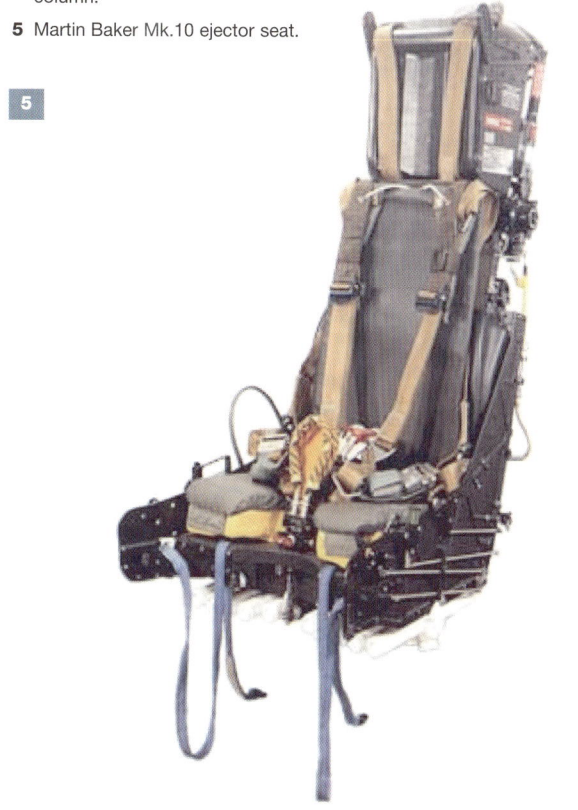

5 Martin Baker Mk.10 ejector seat.

5 Mirage F1 In Detail – Spanish Mirage F1M

1 This pilot from *Ala 14* of the *Ejercito del Aire* is getting ready to depart on another air-defence mission. This photo provides some useful detail on the pilotos flying clothing and the Martin Baker ejection seat.

2 Cockpit canopy on a *Ejercito del Aire* Mirage F1M shown in the open position.

3 Another useful shot for those requiring reference material on the type and style of flying clothing worn by *Ejercito del Air* Mirage F1 pilots. Note also the position of the boarding ladder.

4 Close-up view of the warning/status panel fitted just below the head-up display in the Mirage F1M.

5 Close-up of the right-hand side console in the updated Mirage F1M cockpit.

6 Waiting for clearance to depart. This photograph provides some useful references on the upper surfaces of the Martin Baker ejection seat and rear cockpit area along with some of the safety markings displayed on *Ejercito del Aire* Mirages.

5 Mirage F1 In Detail – *Armée de l'Air* Mirage F1B/C/CR/CT

1. Capitaine Didier Cohendet appears to be quite happy as he prepares to depart for another sortie during the 2001 NATO Tiger Meet at Kleine Brogel. His tiger-striped helmet contrasts nicely with the rather drab surroundings of a military cockpit. Of particular note in this view is the top box of the Martin Baker Mk.10 ejection seat, which features some prominent canopy breakers, not found on the seat fitted to the rear cockpit.

2. This photograph shows a 'crewing-in' prior to the beginning of a sortie, provides a wealth of detailed reference, particularly for the diorama builder. Of note are the position of the two cockpit access ladders, which are two different styles and appropriately decorated for the NATO Tiger Meet, and the placing of the pilot's helmet on the edge of the forward windscreen. For this sortie, *EC5/330* were flying a Dutch F-16 pilot in the backseat so the Mirage pilot is going through the emergency drills and pointing out the key elements of the rear cockpit for the benefit of his 'passenger'. Note also the position of the various warning markings on the forward fuselage and air intakes and the shape of the light fairing which appears to be considerably different from that found on the single-seat variants.

3/4. Capitaine 'Theo' Fontaine of *EC5/330* prepares for another sortie in his Mirage F1CT during the 2001 NATO Tiger Meet at Kleine Brogel. Like his counterparts on the unit he sports an appropriately decorated 'Bone Dome'. These photographs also provide some useful reference material on the upper section of the Martin Baker Mk.10FM ejection seat fitted to the F1CT, the cockpit coaming and canopy.

5. Capitaine 'Theo' Fontaine completes a post-flight de-brief with one of the groundcrew from *EC5/330*. This photograph provides some valuable references on the design of *Armée de l'Air* fast-jet pilot clothing and safety equipment. Note also the arrangement for mounting the cockpit access ladder on the Mirage F1 single-seat variants.

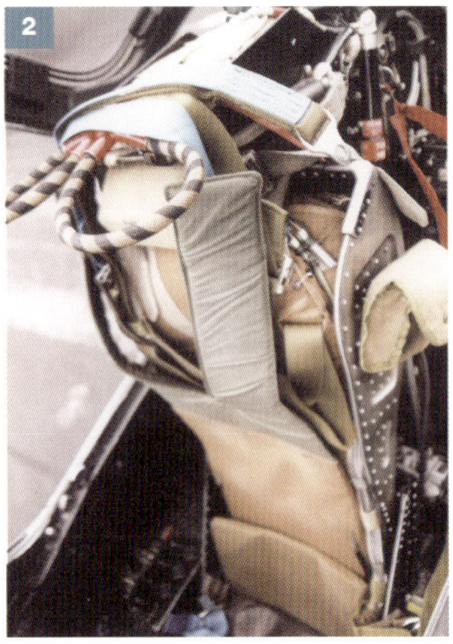

5 Mirage F1 In Detail – *Armée de l'Air* Mirage F1B/C/CR/CT

1 A close-up view of the top section of the Mk.4 seat, showing the position of the firing handle and the shoulder straps, which are Tan and Medium Blue in colour.

2 Upper section of the Martin Baker Mk.4 seat, showing the pattern and colouring of the lumbar support, which is Light Tan and Olive Green. Note also the extremely worn appearance of the main seat frame which has had most of its Satin Black finish worn away to natural metal and the second set of ejection seat firing handles, situated above head height, which clearly date this particular Ejection seat variant. The positioning of the various shoulder straps, whilst the aircraft is at rest, is also noteworthy.

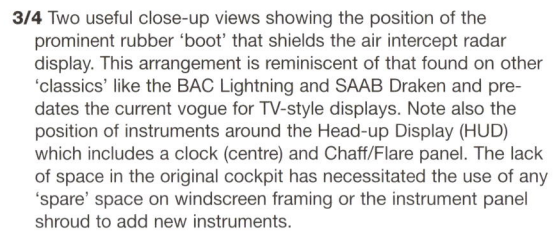

3/4 Two useful close-up views showing the position of the prominent rubber 'boot' that shields the air intercept radar display. This arrangement is reminiscent of that found on other 'classics' like the BAC Lightning and SAAB Draken and pre-dates the current vogue for TV-style displays. Note also the position of instruments around the Head-up Display (HUD) which includes a clock (centre) and Chaff/Flare panel. The lack of space in the original cockpit has necessitated the use of any 'spare' space on windscreen framing or the instrument panel shroud to add new instruments.

5/6 The instrument panel, control column and right hand console of a Mirage F1C cockpit. The instrument panel is a typical Dassault design of the period; functional with small analogue instruments. The primary, Satin Black colour scheme is well worn after thirty years of service. This aircraft also appears to have the original Martin Baker Mk.4 ejection seat fitted to early variants of the F1C. Note the Light Brown/Tan leather seat cushion and the Tan/Medium Blue lap straps and leg restraints.

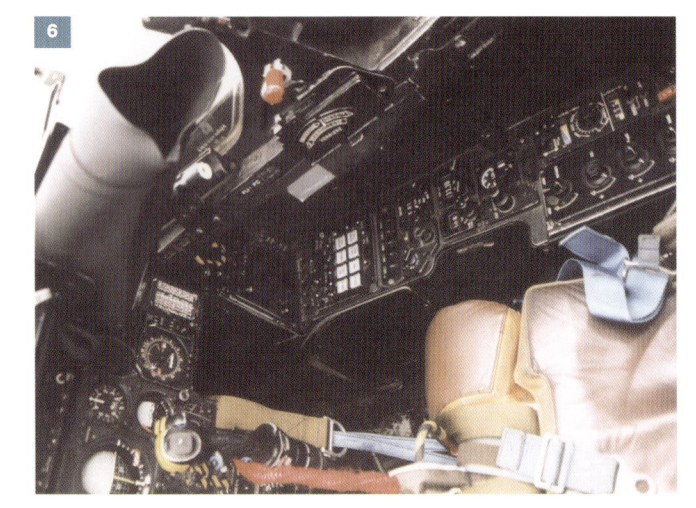

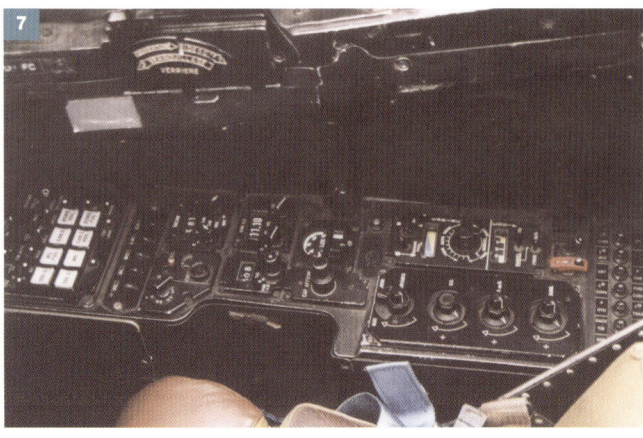

7 Close-up of the relatively simple right-hand cockpit console, which houses a weapons control panel and communications switches amongst others.

5 Mirage F1 In Detail – *Armée de l'Air* Mirage F1B/C/CR/CT

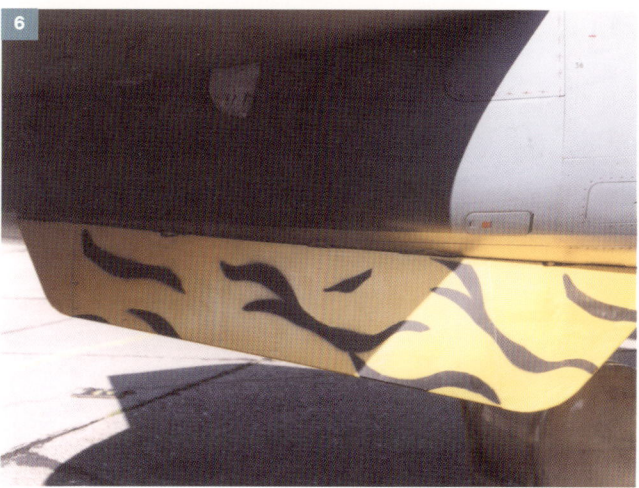

1 General view of the forward fuselage and canopy of the F1B variant clearly showing the style of codes found on *Armée de l'Air* Mirage F1s and the ejection seat warning triangle. Note the arrangement of equipment on the cockpit coaming and the wear and tear around the mounting sockets for the cockpit access ladder.

2 Another view of the forward fuselage, this time on the starboard side which illustrates the position of the two dynamic pressure sensors, to the right of the picture, and the pale yellow blade aerial fitted to the undersurfaces.

3 Close-up of the starboard air intake fairing and ejection seat warning triangle.

4 Close-up of the zap that appears on the starboard air intake, which differs in style from that found on the opposite side of this particular aircraft.

5 Special marking applied to the port air intake of the F1B.

6 The ventral strakes of 330-AD/513 did not escape the attentions of the Aircraft Spray shop at Mont-de-Marsan and were also appropriately decorated with Black and Yellow tiger stripes.

7 The port fin surfaces of the same aircraft featured the markings of the second Flight to make up *EC5/330*, *SPA 163* 'Siberian Tigers'. Both unit insignia had been in unauthorised use for a number of years before becoming officially recognised in October 2000.

75

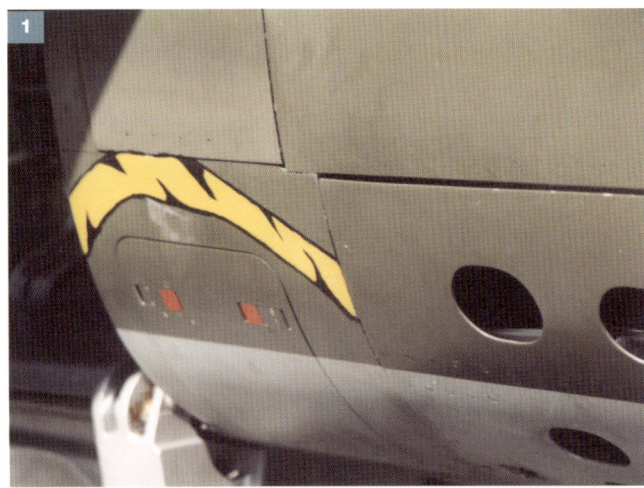

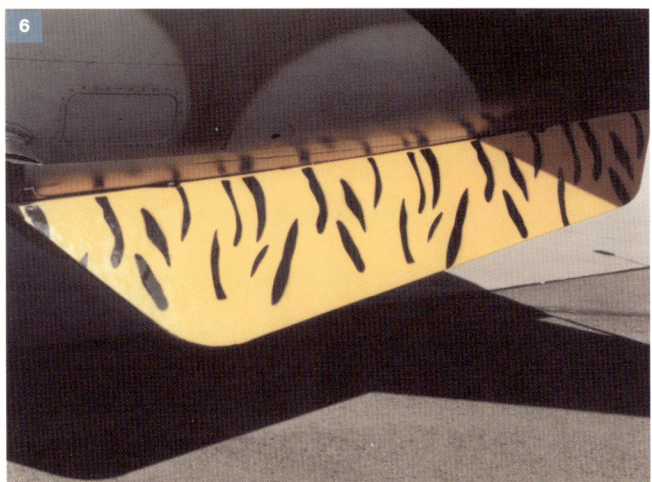

5 Mirage F1 In Detail – *Armée de l'Air* Mirage F1B/C/CR/CT

1. This tiger's tail appears to be 'trapped' between the starboard air brake housing and the main undercarriage bay!

2. This very colourful tiger's head motif contrasts sharply with the camouflage applied to the starboard 1200 litre RP-35 drop tank.

3. Close-up of the leading edge of the port air brake clearly showing the shape of the apertures that adorn the door assembly. Note the green markings applied to various access doors to denote their function.

4. Detailed view of the tiger's head motif applied to the port 1200 litre drop tank.

5. Even the outer fins of the 1200 litre RP-35 drop tanks received attention, with some appropriate tiger striping applied in high-visibility Yellow and Black.

6. Towards the rear of the aircraft, the outer surfaces of the ventral strakes were also subjected to the Yellow and Black airbrushes of the Aircraft Spray Shop at Mont-de-Marsan. Note the fuel dump pipe at the extreme left hand side of this view.

7. The port fin surfaces of F1CR 330-AF/605 carried this tiger and 'pin-up' motif together with 'Lechfeld 98' titles.

5 Mirage F1 In Detail – *Armée de l'Air* Mirage F1B/C/CR/CT

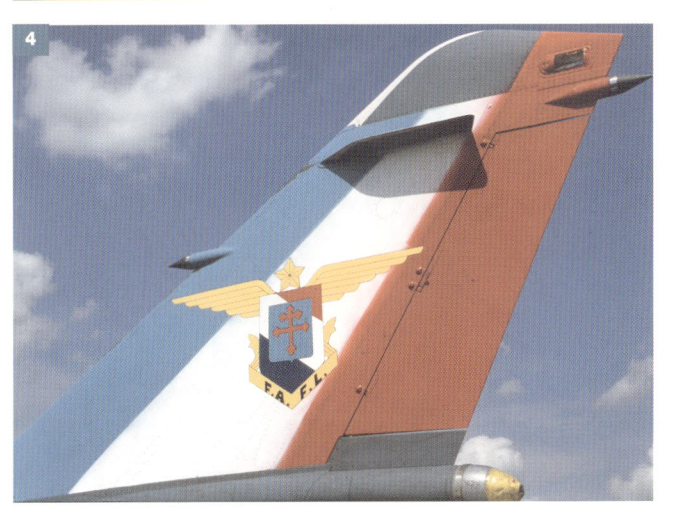

1 A view of the fin surfaces of the initial 'baseline' version of the Dassault Mirage F1C. The view, showing the fin markings in close-up, clearly shows the complete lack of any 'bullet' fairings on completely clean fin leading and trailing edges.

2/3 These two views of the special tail markings applied to Dassault Mirage F1C 12-YA/50 of *EC1/12* 'Cambresis' for the 1994 NATO Tiger Meet also clearly illustrate a lack of bullet fairings on this particular aircraft.

4 By contrast, the specially marked fin of this Mirage F1C shows the presence of the two 'bullet' fairings fitted to all *Armée de l'Air* Mirage F1Cs from serial No.79 onwards.

5 Close-up of the tail markings applied to F1CR 330-AF/605. The F1CR is fitted with the standard Thomson-CSF BF Radar Warning Receiver units, housed in the two bullet shaped fairings on the leading and trailing edge of the fin. Note also the small air intake located on the upper rear fuselage in the middle of the photograph.

6/7 Close-up of the tiger caricature that was applied to the starboard air intake of F1CR 330-AF/605 apparently being sucked into the engine. Note also the retractable landing light fairing and how this differs from that found on the port intake.

77

5 Mirage F1 In Detail – *Armée de l'Air* Mirage F1B/C/CR/CT

1 This photograph, taken from an interesting angle, provides some valuable references for the 1200 litre drop tank and the special markings applied to it. Note also the position of the cockpit canopy.

2 Close-up view of the upper spine area immediately aft of the cockpit, showing the red navigation light fairing and the style of rescue arrow marking applied to most *Armée de l'Air* Mirage F1s.

3 The special tiger markings applied to F1CR 330-AT/655 for Nato Tiger Meet 2002 included some multi-coloured tiger stripes on the leading edges and sides of the port air intake as seen in this view. Note in particular the style of the ejection seat warning triangles and other emergency/rescue markings that differ from those found on earlier F1B and F1C variants.

4 Close-up of the smiling tiger caricature that adorned the starboard fin surfaces of Mirage F1CR 330-AT/655.

5 The port fin surfaces of the same aircraft sported an angry tiger caricature, complete with a typically Gallic red beret, strangling a duck. The significance of this marking cannot be explained.

6 Close-up of a 'zap' that appears on the air intake of at least one *Armée de l'Air* Mirage F1 during the 2001 NATO Tiger Meet at Kleine Brogel.

5 Mirage F1 In Detail – *Armée de l'Air* Mirage F1B/C/CR/CT

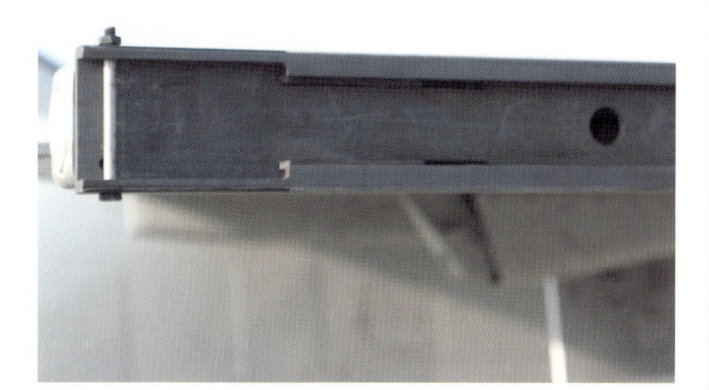

1 *Armée de l'Air* Mirage F1s are equipped with the MATRA Phimat chaff dispenser shown here, fitted to an Alkan pylon on the Starboard outer stores station. This highly effective combat-proven dispenser has seen widespread service on a range of European combat aircraft including *Armée de l'Air* Jaguars and Royal Air Force Harrier GR7s, Jaguars GR1/3s and Tornado F3s. The disruptive pattern camouflage scheme applied to this pod is noteworthy.

2 Barax ECM pod fitted to the starboard outer wing stores pylon. The pod is principally finished in silver.

3 A close-up view of the ASTAC Pod – a belly-mounted electronic intelligence pod which detects and confirms the presence of air-defence radars. It can be fitted to every tactical aircraft in the current *Armée de l'Air* inventory but is extensively used by the Dassault Mirage F1 fleet. (Photo: via ASTAC/The Aviation Workshop Archives)

4/5 Two useful close-up views of the wingtip missile pylon fitted to the F1.

6 A useful close-up photograph of the Raphael-TH Side-Looking Airborne Radar (SLAR) pod fitted to a heavily laden Mirage F1CR, which is also carrying drop tanks and a Phimat Chaff/Flare dispenser. The Raphael-TH system has been used extensively during operations in the Middle East, Gulf and Balkans. (Photo: Aviation Workshop 'Gulf War' Photo Collection)

79

Bibliography

Books

Attrill, Mark P. (2003). *Dressed to Kill.* (Shrewsbury, England: Airlife Publishing)

Attrill, Mark P. (1997). *Tiger ! Tigre ! Tigros! – The Squadrons of the NATO Tiger Association.* (Shrewsbury, England: Airlife Publishing)

Auger, Philippe and Vergeneres, Frederic (2003). *Check List No.1 – AMD-BA Mirage F1.* (Clichy-la-Garenne, France: Editions DTU)

Ávila, Gonzalo and Yáñez, Roberto (2001). *Dassault Mirage F1.* (Barcelona, Spain: Reserva Anticipada Ediciones)

Bishop, Chris, ed (1997). *The Aerospace Encyclopaedia of Air Warfare Volume II.* (London: Aerospace Publishing)

Bishop, Farzad and Cooper, Tom (2003). *Iranian F-4 Phantom II Units in Combat* – Osprey Combat Aircraft No.37. (Oxford: Osprey Publishing)

Duchateau, Philippe and Huertas, Salvador Mafé. (1990). *Mirage! 'Dassault's Mach 2 Warriors'* – Osprey Colour Series. (London, England: Osprey Publishing)

Eagle Press (1996). *NATO's First Blood: Air War Over Bosnia.* (Hong Kong: Concord Publications)

Francillon, Rene (1986). *Dassault Mirage F1* – Aerofax Minigraph No.17. (USA)

Green, William and Swanborough, Gordon. *Flying Colours.* Salamander Books

Guyot, Henri (1991). *La Victoire Venue du Ciel, L'Armée de l'Air au Moyen-Orient.* (France: Lavauzelle Publications)

Jackson, Paul (1985). *Mirage – Military Combat Aircraft Number 23.* (London: Guild Publishing)

Lord, Dick (2000). *Vlamgat – The story of the Mirage F1 in the South African Air Force.* (Pretoria: Covos-Day)

Lord, Dick (2003). *From Tailhooker to Mudmover – An aviation career in the Royal Naval Fleet Air Arm, United States Navy and South African Air Force.* (Irene, South Africa: Corporal Publications)

Micheletti, Eric (1991). *Air War over the Gulf – Europa Militaria No.8.* (London, England: Windrow and Greene Ltd)

Micheletti, Eric (1991). *'Operation Daguet' – French Air Force in the Gulf War.* (Hong Kong: Concord Publications)

Morse, Stan, ed (1991). *Gulf Air War Debrief* – World Air Power Journal Special. (London: Aerospace Publishing)

Nachbauer, Christian and Vivier, Dominique, eds (1998). *La Force Aerienne Tactique 1965–1994.* (Dinsheim: Association Point Fixe)

Parotte, Claude (2003). *Les Ailes Françaises de 1990–2002.* (France: Edition Imprimerie Valettoise)

Ripley, Tim (1996). *Air War Bosnia.* (Shrewsbury, England: Airlife Publishing)

Ripley, Tim (2001). *Conflict in the Balkans 1991–2000* – Osprey Combat Aircraft No.24. (Oxford: Osprey Publishing)

Stafrace, Charles. *Arab Air Forces.* (USA: Squadron Signal Publications)

Journals and Periodicals

Caruana, Richard J (2003). *Mirage F1 Exports.* Scale Aviation Modeller International Volume 9 Issue 8 August 2003. pp.735–742

Debay, Yves (1997). *Mirage over the Savannah* – World Air Power Journal Volume 30. (London: Aerospace Publishing)

Gasztych, Christophe and Vinot-Prefontaine, Benjamin (2004). *Mirage F1CT Aircraft Profile.* Air Forces Monthly February 2004. pp.58–63

IPMS (UK), *Gulf War Special Interest Group Newsletter No.2 and 3.*

Jackson, Paul (1994). *Dassault Mirage F1 Gallic Guardian* – World Air Power Journal Volume 17. (London: Aerospace Publishing)

Klaus, David H. (1988). *IPMS Color Cross Reference Guide.* (USA)

Lake, Jon (2001). *Dassault Mirage F1 Armée de l'Air versions* – International Air Power Review Volume 1. (London: Airtime Publishing)

Nachbauer, Christian, Stollesteiner, Jean-Yues and Vivier, Dominique (2002). *Point Fixe Magazine.*

Ripley, Tim (1995). *NATO Strikes Back* – World Air Power Journal Volume 22. (London: Aerospace Publishing)

Ripley, Tim (1996). *Operation Crecerelle* – World Air Power Journal Volume 25. (London: Aerospace Publishing)

Scale Aircraft Modelling – various issues

Stijger, Eric (2000). *Formula One* – Aircraft Illustrated Magazine – August 2000. (London: Ian Allan Publishing)

Abbreviations

AAM – Air-to-Air Missile
AB – Air Base
ACF – *Avion de Combat Futur*
AFVG – Anglo-French Variable Geometry
BAC – British Aircraft Corporation
CEAM – *Centre d' Expérimentations Aériennes Militaires*
CEV – *Centre d'Essais en Vol*
CIA – Central Intelligence Agency
DAS – Defensive Aids Suite
D/F – Direction Finding
EC – *Escadre de Chasse*
ECM – Electronic Countermeasures
ECTT – *Escadre de Chasse Touts Temps*
ER – *Escadre de Reconnaissance*
FAE – *Fuerza Aerea Ecuatoriana*
FNLA – *Frente Nacional de Libertaçao de Angola*
FS – Federal Standards
GBU – Guided Bomb Unit
HUD – Head-up Display
IAI – Israel Aircraft Industries
IFOR – Implementation Force
IFR – In-flight Refuelling
LGB – Laser-guided Bomb
LTV – Ling Temco Vought
MRCA – Multi-role Combat Aircraft
NATO – North Atlantic Treaty Organisation
OCU – Operational Conversion Unit
RAF – Royal Air Force
RWR – Radar Warning Receiver
SAAF – South African Air Force
SFOR – Stabilisation Force
SNECMA – *Société Nationale d'Etudes et Construction de Moteurs d'Aviation*
UN – United Nations
UNITA – *Uniao Nacional para a Independecia Total de Angola*
VOR – VHF Omni-directional Range